TALKIN'
BIG

TALKIN'
BIG

**How an Iowa Farm Boy Beat the Odds
to Found and Lead One of the
World's Largest Brokerage Firms**

TOM DITTMER

Skyhorse Publishing

Skyhorse Publishing books may be purchased in bulk at special discounts for sales promotion, corporate gifts, fund-raising, or educational purposes. Special editions can also be created to specifications. For details, contact the Special Sales Department, Skyhorse Publishing, 307 West 36th Street, 11th Floor, New York, NY 10018 or info@skyhorsepublishing.com.

Skyhorse® and Skyhorse Publishing® are registered trademarks of Skyhorse Publishing, Inc.®, a Delaware corporation.

www.skyhorsepublishing.com

10 9 8 7 6 5 4 3 2 1

Library of Congress Cataloging-in-Publication Data on file.

Cover design by Brian Peterson
Cover photo credit: Frances Schultz

Print ISBN: 978-1-5107-3705-1
Ebook ISBN: 978-1-5107-3707-5

Printed in the United States of America

CONTENTS

To my wife, Frances;
my son, Jason, and his wife, Allison;
my daughter, Alexis;
and my grandchildren Casey, Jesse, and Piper.

TALKIN'
BIG

1

JUST AN IOWA FARM BOY

W e're going to Portugal to go bird shooting," George Barley said.

"No, George, all we do is shoot, and it costs a fortune!" I told him. "I'm not going. No. Not a chance."

We did it anyway, because George could talk me into just about anything. We stayed at a very nice house in Alentejo, in the cork country. At that time, in the mid '80s, most of the world's cork came from there.

There were sixteen of us in the shooting party: King Constantine II of Greece, his wife Queen Anne-Marie, some of the Hanovers, some of the Hapsburgs, George Barley, and me. All of those European royals are related.

Dinner the first night was held in the wine cellar. Our hosts had invited fourteen of their friends, and we sat at a table long enough to seat all thirty of us. Behind each of our chairs stood a footman ready to wait on us. From one end of the table to the other were piles of fresh shellfish. At each place setting were two silver buckets, one for the shells, and one for the wine. The footmen emptied our shells and refilled our glasses frequently.

The next morning the men went shooting, and the women followed later in horse-drawn carriages. We all met in the field for elevenses, which is a light snack and tea served at eleven o'clock. Then we all returned to the house, where we had drinks outside under the trees and waited for lunch. Suddenly these amazing, fancy white horses began trotting out, and I couldn't believe it. They were the Lipizzan stallions! Honest to God, it was the Spanish Riding School of Vienna. The Hapsburgs, relatives of some in our shooting party, developed the Lipizzan breed in the sixteenth century.

I was blown away. I had never seen anything like it in my life. I had never had dinner with a king, with a footman at each chair; I had never had elevenses; and I had never been to a lunch where the Spanish Riding School was the entertainment.

Hey! I'm just an Iowa farm boy.

2

THE EARLY DAYS

My mother, Evelyn Jewel Robertson, lived with her mother, father, brothers, and sister on a farm in Hawarden, Iowa, near the South Dakota border. When my mother was thirteen years old, her mother died of a heart attack. Her older sister, Irene, had left the farm and moved to Kentucky to get married, and that left my mother to cook three meals a day and do the laundry for her family and the hired hands, all while attending school. She rode a horse to a one-room schoolhouse early every morning, and those Midwestern winters were cold!

A few years later, Mother met Marlin Dittmer, who lived with his Aunt Myrtle in Ireton, a few miles down the road. Marlin's mother had died soon after he was born, and his father was killed in a car accident when Marlin was thirteen. Marlin was three years older than my mother and hadn't had much guidance in life. He was a drinker and a bad boy, which my mother liked. She also liked the idea of getting off the farm.

They had sex once and she became pregnant at sixteen. They got married because that's just what you did then. She was seventeen when I was born and she never graduated from high school. The year was 1942. Marlin left soon after my birth to join the Navy, and my mother and I moved into a small apartment above a dry cleaner in Hawarden.

My parents divorced by the time I was a year old. As it turned out, I would only see Marlin a few times in my life. The concept of being raised by a single parent never occurred to me as a child, though. The biggest stigma my mother was forced to endure came when she had to go on welfare for six months. They called it "subsistence" then, and nobody talked about it much in those days. How poor were you that you were taking money from the government? God, it was the worst and it was shameful. She was finally able to go off subsistence after she got a job at the dry cleaners downstairs.

When I was just a year old, I contracted polio, though it wasn't properly diagnosed at the time. They thought I had pediatric rheumatoid arthritis. I cried constantly and I couldn't walk like a one-year-old should be able to. My legs hurt, my knees were swollen, and every night my mother put hot packs on my legs to try to ease the pain. By the time I was three, it just went away. Ten years later, they diagnosed me as having non-paralytic polio. Fortunately, the only effect that lingered was on my running. I was never fast. When I was in the Army, I could jog up to twelve miles with a heavy pack on my back, but if I had to sprint, I was slow.

I started stuttering from the time I could talk. Everyone in my family said, "Oh, he thinks faster than he can speak." It wasn't until I went to school that the teasing started.

I remember going a couple of times to visit with Aunt Myrtle and Grandpa Dittmer, and to see Marlin, in Le Mars, about thirty miles away. Aunt Myrtle was an old maid who lived to be 103. Grandpa Dittmer was seventy-five years older than I was to the day. He was the only one on Marlin's side of the family that my mother really liked. She thought he was a wonderful man.

Grandpa Dittmer came to Iowa in 1860, right before the start of the Civil War. He built four farms and became rich. Before the Depression, he sold his farms to his relatives, but they stiffed him on the deals because no one had any money.

One summer when I was about five, Marlin came to visit me for about an hour. Just before he left, he told me, "I'll send you a red cowboy suit."

I went home and told my mother, "I'm going to get a red cowboy suit." And for one year I asked about that cowboy suit every single day. Finally, my mother, who had no extra money, bought one and said it was from him. It wasn't until I was an adult that I found out that she just couldn't take my disappointment. I didn't see Marlin again until I was eighteen.

That was when I began to understand that when you tell someone you're going to do something, you'd better do it.

3

THE FARM

The farm in Hawarden was a big part of my early life. Grandpa Robertson lived on the farm. My aunts, uncles, and eight cousins all lived nearby. We could go to any of the aunts' and uncles' houses and have breakfast, lunch, or dinner anytime. The only downside was they would make me take a bath, which I didn't want to do.

We never took a vacation; we just went to the farm and to see our relatives. My mother's sister Irene lived in Kentucky and occasionally we would take the train to visit her. That was a big deal. But every summer we'd all go back to the farm. Sometimes there were three boys in one bed, so it wasn't exactly comfortable on those hot summer nights. There wasn't a bathroom upstairs in the farmhouse, so we were supposed to use the honey pot when nature called. But we didn't. We'd just piss out the window through the screen. Once, Aunt Virginia asked us, "Are you boys peeing out the window?" Oh, no, no, no. Of course there was a big hole in the screen from all the acid in our urine. They changed the screen and threatened to kill us if we ever did it again.

Aunt Irene was married to Ted Newman. Ted's Uncle Charlie was one of those guys afflicted with that disease where he'd say he was going for a pack of cigarettes and be gone for six months. He used shoe polish on his hair so you couldn't tell he was going gray. Charlie was married to a good-looking nurse, and Grandpa Robertson was schtupping her. It was a big scandal.

Charlie would tell us terrifying stories about civet cats that lived in the basement. For extra effect, he would tap on the bottom of the table and move the floorboards with his feet. We were six petrified little boys who wouldn't sleep for days afterward. Then he'd say, "I'm going to get a pack of cigarettes," and he'd be gone again.

All of my cousins smoked, but I never did because my mother smoked and I thought it was disgusting.

When we got older, Uncle Paul would take us coon hunting. He had a dog, Ring, who smelled terrible, and every time Ring saw me, he would jump up on me, knock me over, and lick me. When we'd go hunting, Uncle Paul would holler, "Talk to me, Ring, talk to me." The dog would howl and you could tell by the howl if he was on a scent or had something treed. That howl made the hair on the back of your neck stand up. A full moon on the snow and a howling dog was enough to make you quiver. It scared me to death, but I loved every minute of it. I mean all I did was walk along, colder than hell, but boy, I thought that was heaven. I was out with all the kids and my uncle, coon hunting at night with Ring. That feeling has never left me after all these years.

Paul was a big, good-looking guy, and in the summer he would get out his big bowie knife, point at me, and say, "Anybody want to go fishing? Tom, come here. Let's cut some worm off you so we can go fishing." I was terrified and I'd run like crazy. My mother would get mad at him but everyone else thought it was hysterical. Maybe the fear of Paul trimming my wiener to use for bait is why I hate fishing today.

In the summer we'd shoot squirrels and pull weeds out of the soybeans. There were probably 200 acres of soybeans, and we'd get paid a dime a row. And those were some long rows. In the early mornings, when the adults were in the kitchen making breakfast, we'd go into the garden and eat watermelon and cantaloupe right off the vine. I hated beets, but when you pulled them out of the ground and knocked the dirt off of them, they were juicy and sweet. That's what we had for breakfast most days, and we thought it was great.

On Saturday the whole family would go into town, about fifteen miles away. That was a big event. But first we had to take baths. There was running water in the house, but it was cold, so first you'd have to boil the water on the wood stove. Then, after everyone was clean, we'd jam ourselves into the cars and head into town.

Every Sunday the whole family went to the Baptist Church. My mother used to say, "You know who is sitting in the front row? All those bankers who put all these poor farmers out of business." We kids would tell the adults that we were going to sit in the balcony, and then we'd sneak out and steal Grandpa's car. It was a 1949 Ford, and my job was to lie on the floor in the front seat and hold the foil gum wrapper on the starter so it would start. We could have used a rubber band, but since they had me, that was my job. Then one of the cousins would drive us up and down the alleys, smoking Grandpa's cigarettes, which of course they had also stolen. I thought that was the coolest thing. We'd take the car back to the church, but sometimes we'd have to park in a different spot from where we got it. Grandpa never said a word about the cigarettes or the car.

The outhouse at the farm was a "two-holer." Our toilet paper was pages torn from the Sears and Montgomery Ward catalogs, but we saved the lingerie ads to look at while we were on the john. Then the discussion amongst the boys would revolve around which catalog had the better lingerie section. I always thought it was Montgomery Ward.

One time we thought we saw a nipple—that was good for about a week's discussion.

One day I was down by the creek with my cousins and they were talking about the birds and the bees. They were three or four years older than I was, and they were describing how babies were made, about putting the penis in the lady.

"No, no, no," I said. "My mother told me God puts the seed inside the woman and that's how you get a baby." They all laughed like crazy, so hard they fell over. So later I went to my mother and asked, "Mom, how does the seed get in there?"

"God puts it in there," she said.

"No," I told her. "Roger said that a man sticks his wiener in there, and boom, that's the seed."

"Well, that's how God does it," she said. End of discussion.

That was life on the farm. We'd go back there every summer until I started driving, and then I didn't want to go as much.

4

FATHERS

When I was in first grade, one of the first things I was asked in class was "What does your father do?"

"I don't have a father," I said, and everyone laughed at me. I was humiliated because I didn't know that I had a father.

"You go home and ask your mother," my teacher said.

At that point, I didn't even know fathers, as such, existed. I was never told anything good, bad, or indifferent; Marlin was a non-event. I had my whole family at the farm, and I had my Aunt Myrtle and Grandpa Dittmer on that side of the family. No one really talked about Marlin except for Aunt Myrtle, who would occasionally say he was a wonderful guy.

I went home and talked to my mother. "You never said I had a father," I told her.

"Why are you asking?" she asked me.

"I told them in school that I didn't have a father and they all laughed," I said.

"You have a father," she said.

"Why didn't you tell me?" I asked.

"Because he's not here," she said. And that was that.

It didn't occur to me to ask my mother why he wasn't around anymore. I had a large family, and I felt loved all the time. Hell, I was in good shape.

My mother was strong and meaner than a junkyard dog. She was 6'2", broad shouldered, and at 200 pounds she was skinny. I guess she was pretty, because everyone used to say so. She and Aunt Irene both had very large breasts, and when they would hug me, oh my God, it was the most secure place in the world. It never occurred to me that anything bad could happen to me, so I guess that's why I didn't miss having a father.

There was a bully in my first grade class who always threatened to beat me up. I was small, couldn't run fast, and I stuttered, which made me an easy target. My mother would see me running home from school and ask me why.

"Because the bully is going to beat me up," I said.

"Well," she told me, "tomorrow you're gonna have to confront the bully. Because if you run home again, I'm going to spank you."

When the bully walked out of the schoolhouse the next day, I popped him, and he beat the shit out of me. But then he wanted to be my best friend. After that I got to walk home, and I was fine.

5

SIOUX CITY

My mother needed to earn more money, so we moved to Sioux City when I was in the third grade. On the first day of school they asked me my name and I sang it, because for some reason stutterers are able to sing their words without stuttering. Then they asked me why I was singing. So, instead of singing, I stuttered out my name, which made a terrible first impression on my new classmates. I never volunteered to speak up in class again. I didn't know the answers anyway, because I had a hard time reading, but even if I had known the answers they would have been too hard for me to get out.

Every day at two o'clock they would come and get me and take me to the Special Ed class. There was a girl with Down's syndrome, one or two other boys with special needs, and me. Being eight years old and in a Special Ed class every day for stuttering did not, unfortunately, help me with my stuttering. There wasn't a day that my being collected for Special Ed wasn't followed by a snicker in my classroom.

I didn't have any friends when we first moved to Sioux City, so I usually played alone after school. The apartment where we lived had a ledge that ran all around the building. It was about six feet off the ground, and I would walk around that ledge pretending it was very dangerous and I was a hero rescuing some damsel in distress. It was a huge deal to me to be a hero.

The worst thing I remember about that first year in Sioux City was when my mother gave me a dollar and asked me to go to the store to buy her some thread. Somewhere along the way I lost the dollar, and when I went home and told her, she cried. My mother was not a crier. Losing a dollar was a very big deal because even though my mother worked all day long there was never any money left.

By the time that I went to North Junior High, I had made a few friends. I was never a very good athlete, and I was still small for my age because I was always sick. They finally took out my tonsils when I was fifteen, and I grew six or seven inches in one year and then kept growing all the way through college. I was an inch taller when I graduated college than I was when I enrolled. As in elementary school, I still had trouble reading and I still stuttered, but the kids weren't making fun of me anymore. Well, one still was: the preacher's son. We were in ninth grade, and he was a big kid for his age. I hit him once, and he hit me back so hard he knocked me over the bicycle rack. Then he helped me up and said, "That's enough. We're going to be best friends." But I didn't want to be his best friend because I thought he was a schmuck.

When television came to Sioux City, TV trays and Swanson's TV dinners came out. If the adults were there, something good was on TV, and the rabbit ears didn't work, I'd have to put aluminum foil on the antennae and stand there and hold them. It was the same deal as lying on the floor of my grandpa's car and holding the foil on the starter. Ed Sullivan was big back then, and so was Sid Caesar. There weren't many shows, and they came on at five o'clock and ended at nine. TV was a big deal.

When I was in junior high school, my mother worked successively as a waitress at the Turn Inn, then at a deli, and then as a checker in the grocery store. She'd be at work all day, and when I came home from school there would always be a list of things she wanted me to do to keep busy and out of trouble: wash dishes, dust, vacuum, and anything else she could think of. When she came home there would be an inspection. Every now and then I'd lift up the rug and push a little dirt under it, but she always found it. She gave me the chores because she wanted me home and not hanging around someplace else. Even though she was busy working, she knew where I was every hour of the day.

My mother and I were a family, and she was as affectionate with me as she was tough on me. We ate dinner every night at home and had breakfast together every morning. Then she would go off to work and I would go to school. We didn't have much, but I never thought about money. I was never hungry and most of the time I thought life was great.

I worked in the cafeteria in junior high and all the way through high school so that I could get a free thirty-five-cent lunch. I washed dishes and did anything else they wanted me to do. The only good thing about it, besides the free lunch, was that I always had clean hands. They looked like prunes at the end of the day, but they were clean.

When I was thirteen, I took some little boy's candy at Halloween. The boy told his mother, and she called mine. As I was coming home that day, I saw my mother waiting for me on the steps. "What?" I asked.

"You bullied that little boy and took his candy. I'm so disgusted with you that I can't stand it. Come here!" she demanded.

I started running, but she chased me. Boom. We were in the front yard, where everyone could see. She grabbed me and spanked the living shit out of me right there.

"Now, get outta my sight," she said. "Get in the house and go to bed." Ooh, she was mad, but I deserved it.

One day, when I was fourteen, I was riding my bike down this big hill. At the bottom of the hill sat the store where my mother worked as a checker. I always rode down that hill as fast as I could. To make the corner at the bottom, I'd lean my bike all the way over and just keep going. It just so happened that on that day, at that exact moment, a lady came out of the grocery store holding a bag in each arm. Her back was to me as I was racing down the hill, and as I passed her, my handlebar grazed one of the bags. The bag flipped up and the groceries went flying. Her bread landed on the hood of her car, and a bottle of Clorox flew up into the air and smashed on the ground. I kept going for about a half a block, and I was laughing so hard that I literally fell off my bike onto someone's lawn. After a couple of minutes, I got back on my bike and went back to see if the lady was okay.

When I arrived on the scene there was a big commotion, and the store manager was out there with the lady.

"What happened?" I asked.

"I think my Clorox exploded," she said.

"Oh, I've heard of that before," I said. Yeah, right.

The store manager looked at her like she was crazy.

"Lady," he said, "Clorox doesn't explode."

"Well, mine did!" she said.

And I, ever helpful, said, "I've heard of that before!"

Luckily my mother didn't see any of this!

Once, when I was fifteen, I stole my mother's car. You'd think I would have learned by that time not to mess with her. She had gone out with some friends, and I just decided to take her car. I drove around on back roads so no one would see me. I came home and pulled her car back into the garage and wiped it down so it was spotless. But now I was worried, so at about five o'clock I got out the push mower and started mowing the lawn. By the time I was finished and went back inside, my mother was sitting at the kitchen table drinking a cup of coffee.

"Do you have anything you want to tell me?" she asked me.

I start crying right away. "I stole the car!"

"That's fine," she says, "I know."

"How?"

"I've been looking at you for the last few months," she said, "and I knew you were going to steal the car. So every day I made a chalk mark behind the tire. And I knew that if that chalk mark wasn't there, you took the car. Now if you had lied to me, you wouldn't have liked it. You wouldn't be out of this house again for six months. But you didn't lie. It's over. And don't ever do it again."

6

SIXTEEN

I got my driver's license at sixteen, and I really wanted a car. My mother said if I got a B average in school and no Ds, somehow we'd get a car. I found school to be really hard because I was a slow reader. In those days, dyslexia and reading problems weren't really talked about. Achieving a B average was going to be a challenge for me.

Somehow I did it. My mother looked at me and said, "Why were you getting Ds and Fs for all this time, and then, when there's a car involved, you get all Bs?"

"Because I really want the car," I told her.

I had a little money saved up, and with my mother's help we bought a used 1955 Ford two-door for $500. It was so cool. It had a black interior with ugly, multi-colored seat covers, but I didn't care. I loved it. After a while I earned more money and put on dual exhaust pipes.

I worked after school and on weekends at Chef Burger in Sioux City. Then, the summer after I turned sixteen, I got a job unloading trucks for American Produce. I worked twelve hours a day for $1 an hour, but on Saturday I earned $1.50 an hour, and on Sunday $2.

I could make $1,000 working three months in the summer. That was a lot of money in those days, especially for a family like ours.

American Produce sold eggs to companies like Kraft Foods and Pillsbury. They sold frozen whites and frozen yolks separately, sugared, salted, or plain. Those kinds of businesses no longer exist today because today the baking companies do it all themselves.

My job was to unload cartons from the trucks and take them into the cooler. When the eggs were needed, I'd go into the cooler, load up a dolly, and take them into the egg-breaking room. The women in the egg-breaking room were from the Winnebago tribe of Native Americans. There would be fifty of them lined up in front of a conveyor belt, and they'd take the eggs and break them on a blade. The yolk would fall into a cup under the blade, and the whites would run off. They'd tap the cup and it would pop the yolk into a bucket to be frozen. The whites would go via a vacuum tube into a tank to be mixed with sugar or salt, then separated into buckets for freezing. I'd take the full buckets into the freezer, where the eggs would be flash frozen. I'd just be wearing a T-shirt but I'd have a pair of heavy gloves on. Otherwise my hands would stick to things and tear the skin off. If I worked fast enough, I didn't get cold.

Every now and then I'd walk into the cooler and catch people having sex on top of the egg cartons. Then the women would tease me: "You want to get some of this, honey?" Oh, no, thank you. They thought it was funnier than I did.

The scariest thing that happened was when one of the truck drivers thought he'd have a little fun with me. I had bent down to get a box of eggs off the floor, and he put his boot on my head, pinning me down. I said, "What are you doing?" as I tried to move my head out from under his foot. Another guy, Jerry Grover, came over and said, "Leave him alone." They had words, and Jerry Grover beat the shit out of him—I mean, something terrible. And when the truck driver was splayed out on the floor, Jerry cut him with a church key, the kind used to open beer cans. Then the fellas sprinkled a little sawdust over the bloody spots on the floor and we all went back to work. Needless to say, the guy didn't bother me again.

The next summer, when I turned seventeen, I got a job digging ditches for Iowa Public Service, earning $1.75 an hour. I would also get overtime. Anything over forty hours was double time, which was big.

I had a lot of girlfriends in high school, but I never dated any one girl more than about three times because I didn't want to be rejected. I'd finally gotten taller, but I still stuttered. I was at the bottom of my class. I had a letterman's jacket but no letter. I had no prospects and no money except for what I'd saved from my summer job. Why would anyone go out with me? I still haven't been able to figure that out.

I always wanted to go with the other guys up to Lake Okoboji at Arnolds Park. That was where they had the amusement park with a Ferris wheel, beer joints, and girls. But I didn't have a shot at going. My mother had rules and one of her big ones was *Nothing good happens after nine o'clock at night.*

"But Ma," I would say, "everybody else gets to stay out until ten."

"You're not everybody else. You're going to be home at nine."

The school closest to where we lived was a Catholic school. That was a no-go zone because we were Baptists, and there was tremendous prejudice against Catholics in those days. All the guys really wanted to go there anyway because we thought Catholic girls were hot. Later in life, I met guys from the Catholic school and they said, "You guys had all the hot girls at your school." Wherever you weren't, that's where all the hot girls were.

All I thought about back then was girls. One night I had a date with one of the prettiest girls in the school. I didn't know she had a reputation for being fast. We started out at the drive-in but ended up in a cornfield. I got my foot stuck in the steering wheel, and the whole thing was pretty much a disaster, but we had done the deed.

Afterward, we went and got a pizza and some Cokes. I told her how wonderful everything was, and then I took her home. It was my first time, but it wasn't hers. When I got home and walked into the house, my mother asked, "How was it?"

"What?"

"How was sex tonight?"

"Don't be ridiculous," I said as I walked into the bathroom.

I walked out and my mother said, "Well?"

"Mom!"

Years later I asked my mother how she knew I'd had sex that night.

"Easy," she said. "Every other time you came home from a date, you went from the back door to the icebox. That time you went from the back door straight to the bathroom. You were checking to see if everything was in order. So I knew."

7

POP

After losing my virginity, the second biggest thing that happened to me in my sixteenth year was Ray Friedman. My mother had never had a man in our house until then. Although I had never seen him, Ray owned American Produce, where I worked in the summers. The facility was located across the street from the deli where my mother worked, and Ray would go in there every day for coffee. I first met him when he came to our apartment to pick my mother up for a date.

"You want a cigarette?" he asked me.

"No," I said. "I'm sixteen. I don't smoke."

"Oh," he said. "Good, yeah, good." He was so nervous.

Pop—as I came to call him—was over six feet tall, had red wavy hair, a dimple on his chin, and a big grin. I liked him instantly. He grew up the son of a Jewish chicken broker in a low-income neighborhood of Sioux City. His parents had taught him the chicken and egg business, and his friend Ben Shapiro used to say that Pop had been raised in the back of an egg truck.

When Pop grew up, he bought a used egg truck and created American Produce. One of the things his company did was supply chickens to US servicemen stationed in Korea. In March 1952, Pop and his three brothers-in-law, who had put in the money to start the business, were indicted for selling Grade B chickens to the Army as Grade A. If there was any cut in the chicken's skin, it was automatically a Grade B. And if someone had a truckload of chickens and just nine or ten of them had tiny cuts in their skin, the whole truckload was to be counted legally as Grade B. Pop and his brothers-in-law didn't think that was fair.

Even so, Pop's lawyers told him to plead guilty. They thought the judge would just give him a slap on the wrist and maybe a fine. But instead the judge decided to make an example of Pop. "You're trying to poison our men in the armed services," the judge said. "You're going to go to jail for five years." He also fined Pop $10,000 and paroled the three brothers-in-law. Pop was sent to Leavenworth, went through a series of unsuccessful legal appeals, and ended up in a prison in Seagoville, Texas. Turns out the judge was completely anti-Semitic. They even had him on tape saying things like "I'll teach that kike sonofabitch," but for whatever reason that was never allowed into the court record.

After serving out his sentence, Pop returned home broke, with no job, and his wife on the verge of leaving him for a neighbor. For a while he sold neckties door-to-door, but then he went back to selling eggs for $100 a week.

Prison had a big effect on Pop. He came back a man looking for a fight. For years he wore sunglasses all day, all night, all the time, unless he was sleeping. I think it was psychological. In sunglasses he could be somewhere else. He could escape. He never talked too much about the time he spent in prison, and I could understand that.

Pop had two daughters from his first marriage. Lisette was little and blond, and Linda was tall—almost six feet—and redheaded. She looked exactly like Pop. He and Mother put pressure on me to take Linda out. I didn't want to but I did it anyway. We went to dinner but there was no romantic stuff. When she was in her forties, Linda was diagnosed with bone cancer. Lisette was going to be Linda's bone marrow donor until Pop told her he wasn't Linda's father. Linda was the neighbor's child and not Pop's, even though she looked more like him than Lisette did. Pop and his wife got divorced soon after Linda was born, but Pop raised her as his own. He never said a word to anyone about Linda's true paternity until she got cancer.

In 1959, the summer before my senior year, my mother thought it was time she and Pop got married. He told her he couldn't marry her because she was a shiksa (meaning a Gentile woman) and his entire family was Orthodox Jews.

"Fine," my mother told him. "And, by the way, Tom and I are moving to Las Vegas on the twenty-first of August. I've got a good job there." She didn't make idle threats. When she said she was going to do something, she did it. So we drove to Las Vegas, unloaded the U-Haul, and I started my senior year at Las Vegas High School.

After a week or two, Pop came out to find us. He and my mother got married in Las Vegas, and then we loaded up the U-Haul and drove back to Sioux City in September, less than a month after we'd departed.

Back in Sioux City, we moved into Pop's house on Cheyenne Boulevard, a nice little three-bedroom house with one of the bedrooms serving as Pop's office. Pop's dad was living in California in an old folks, home at the time. When Pop and my mother got married, she told him, "Ray, we don't do that in our family. They come live with us." That's why we had three generations living on the farm together at one time. So Grandpa moved in and took my room and I moved down into the basement. Grandpa was in bad shape when he first arrived. No one thought he would live for more than six months, yet he ended up living close to ten years.

Clare was our maid. My mother would always clean the house before Clare came so she wouldn't think we were sloppy. Clare was pretty cute and Grandpa liked her. "I'll give you a dollar," he'd tell her at least once a day, "if you'll sit on my lap."

"Okay," Clare would tell him, "but you have to give me the dollar first."

So Grandpa would give Clare the dollar, and she would put it in a jar on top of the icebox. By the time she went back to Grandpa, he would have forgotten about the whole transaction. Pop would have to supply Grandpa with dollars about once a week when Grandpa asked for some walking around money. It was a running joke because we knew the money was for Clare, and Pop was giving Grandpa the same dollars every week from the same jar. He was a character.

When I was eighteen, Pop took me to see Marlin. I hadn't seen him since I was a little kid. We were driving to Omaha in Pop's gray 1952 Pontiac to catch a plane to Phoenix. Pop was a big guy and I was a decent size at the time myself. The seats in the car weren't connected and we were sitting so far down that Pop could hardly see over the steering wheel, but he was grinning and flying down the highway at a hundred miles an hour. I looked at him and said, "You always seem so happy. You've been to prison, and you've lost all your money. You've been through a lot. Why are you so happy?"

"It's easy," he said. "You gotta pick happy or sad. I suggest you pick happy."

I laughed and said, "You're right. Pick happy."

We got to Phoenix about dinnertime and walked into the restaurant that Marlin owned. Pop asked the waiter, "Is Marlin Dittmer here?"

"Yes," the waiter told Pop. "He's back in the office."

"Tell him to come out," Pop said. "I want him to meet his son."

After about ten minutes, Marlin peeked out from around the corner and then came out to greet us. We ate and made small talk. Then Pop and I went to the hotel, and the next day we went back to Marlin's for about an hour. We talked about Aunt Myrtle and Grandpa Dittmer for a while, and that was it.

The next time I heard from Marlin was when I made the *Forbes 400* list, sometime in the early '80s. He wanted me to buy him a house. I didn't do it because my mother would have had a fit. The next time I saw Marlin was the one time he came to Lake Forest. And the last time I saw him was when I went down to Phoenix after hearing that he had pancreatic cancer. He picked me up at the airport, we spent a little time together, and then I went home. He died three weeks later. I never really knew him, but that was his choice.

8

GET YOUR ACT TOGETHER

It was the end of my senior year, and I was getting dressed up and ready to take my date to the prom when my mother said to me, "You know, your date is going to want to have sex tonight, and if she gets pregnant, it's going to ruin the rest of your life." Thanks, Mom.

We left the prom at about midnight to go park and neck. As we were driving down the road I looked over and my date was taking her clothes off. So I pulled the car over into a cornfield. I'd only had sex twice before, but I was thinking, *Yes! This is going to happen!* But it didn't. All I could hear was my mother's voice in my head saying, "If she gets pregnant, it's going to ruin the rest of your life." And I lost my nerve.

I graduated high school second from the bottom of my class.

"Son," my mother asked me, "Is there anybody in class who is worse than you are?"

"Yes," I told her. "Beverly Bilbo."

And my mother said, "But son, Beverly Bilbo has Down's syndrome."

★★★

It was 1960 and I was determined to enroll at the University of Iowa, but my grades were so poor that I had to go to summer school before they would admit me in the fall. I took twelve hours of courses that summer and flunked out.

Driving home from Iowa City on Highway 20, it was storming and blowing so hard that the rain came down sideways. I pulled out to pass a station wagon only to find a Studebaker coming right toward me. I stomped on the gas and cut between the Studebaker and the station wagon. The maneuver caused my back bumper to pull the front bumper off the station wagon, and then pull the Studebaker's left front fender off as well as the driver's side door. Out of control, I skidded off the highway and into a ditch. I was lucky that I didn't roll the car. I got out and miraculously I wasn't hurt, because in those days there were no seat belts.

I ran up the road and the driver of the Studebaker, an old man, was just sitting in the driver's seat. His wife was in the front seat, and another lady was in the back seat. They all looked like they were in shock, so I asked if they were okay.

"I don't know," the old guy said. "My fender and my door just fell off."

I was going so fast that he hadn't even seen me. He didn't even know I hit him. He just thought something went wrong with his car and his fender and door had fallen off.

"I thought they made these cars better," he added.

I looked down the road and saw a Navy guy—the driver of the station wagon—coming after me. His wife was hanging onto him, and he was physically dragging her down the road. He was going to kill me, and justifiably so. His kids were also in the car.

Coincidentally, Pop's insurance broker had been in the car behind me, and he quickly intervened before the Navy guy got his hands on me. The police arrived on the scene and found my car in the ditch, totaled. The judge suspended my driver's license for six months, as he should have.

The insurance guy dropped me off at home and told my parents what happened. After he left, I said to my mother, "This was a good omen. No one got hurt and no one got killed." But between the wreck, the totaled car, the terrible grades, and now the flunking out, my mother had had it.

"You're going to go to school, you're going into the Army, or you're getting a job," she said. "That's it. Those are your options."

It was about two in the afternoon, and I went to bed and woke up about forty-eight hours later on a Sunday. I probably got up to pee, but that was it. I could have killed everybody. I had been doing eighty or ninety miles an hour when I hit those cars. I didn't have a scratch on me, but the experience made it clear to me that I needed to get my act together. There was something out there that I was supposed to do.

So I decided I was going to go to the University of South Dakota in Vermillion, some thirty miles away.

"Your high school transcripts look disastrous and you failed out of the University of Iowa summer school. You won't be coming here," said Dr. Frankenthaller, the admissions director.

"Dr. Frankenthaller, I have to come here," I said.

"No, Mr. Dittmer, your grades are too bad."

I was sitting in his waiting room. When he left for the day, I was still sitting there. I went home, got up early the next day and was sitting in his waiting room when he arrived. That night when he left, I was still there. Then I went home, got up early again, and went right back. Finally he said, "Okay, Dittmer, come here." I went into his office, and he said, "We're going to give you the test that we give the Sioux Indians on the reservation. The big question is, do you want to be a plumber or a fireman?" I guess he figured that was the height of my potential. "Pick fireman," he told me. He admitted me into the school, but he was wrong about one thing. Firemen get the girls, but plumbers make the money.

I spent one year at USD and got out with a 3.0 grade point average, which for me was outstanding. After my close call on Highway 20, I knew I had to do something with my life. I think that's why I was so persistent about getting into the University of South Dakota and drove poor Dr. Frankenthaller crazy. I kept that persistence up when I went back to the University of Iowa for my sophomore year, and I guess I never let up.

The biggest thing for me that year in Iowa City was seeing the speech pathologist. The Department of Communication Sciences and Disorders at the university was one of the best in the country at the time. I had been stuttering my whole life and didn't want to do it anymore. The speech pathologist was gorgeous. That was a good sign.

"What's the problem?" she asked me.

"I stutter," I said. "People finish my sentences, and I'd like not to stutter."

"So, what's the problem?" she asked me again.

"Well . . . I stutter." What was wrong with her?

"Look," she said, "if you stopped stuttering today, no one would even notice. That's number one. Number two, they've already accepted you with the stutter and no one is going to mention it to you. Now, tell me the problem." In those years I didn't swear. I didn't even swear when I was in the Army. I actually didn't swear until I reached the trading floor. But when the speech pathologist said that to me, I was thinking plenty of swear words as I got up to leave her office.

I never stuttered again, though. Just like that. I think because, in a roundabout way, she told me I was okay with or without the stutter.

Something just clicked. She was right about people not noticing. At first I would see people on the street and I'd stop and talk to them and I'd think, "Christ, I'm not stuttering." I'd run into someone else and talk to them, not stuttering. Then I started looking for people to talk to. That was it! Never again. ·

I saw my roommate, Corky Kress, every day, and two or three weeks passed before he said, "I guess you're not stuttering anymore, huh?" And that was it. Nobody else said a fucking word! My mother and Pop didn't say anything, the girls I was dating didn't say anything, and my fraternity brothers didn't say anything. As the speech patholo-gist had said, that's who I was and that's who they accepted. It was amazing.

Looking back, stuttering might have been one of the best things that ever happened to me because it forced me to try harder. I might have been good-looking, but I didn't know that. You don't look in the mir-ror when you stutter. Unless I had a pimple or something, I just never looked in the mirror because to me there was nothing to look at. I had to try harder every day just to get along because I stuttered. I think I tried harder my whole life even after I stopped stuttering because I still felt like I was different.

I was majoring in political science but reading was still hard for me and it took me forever. With all my classes in college, I had to read hundreds of pages a week and write papers. I would take my books down to the cafeteria, have dinner, and then take them to the medical library, where I knew I wouldn't run into anyone I knew. It was quiet there, no kids walking in and out, and I could study. On weekdays I would start at six o'clock and end at midnight. I would study most of Saturday and Sunday.

For the first three years, I studied about eighty hours a week just to get Cs. I forced myself to learn how to read. My fraternity brothers took the same classes I did, but they'd never go to class. I didn't cut a class in four years. I'd take a notebook to class and I'd draw a line down the middle of a page. I'd write class notes on one side of the page, then when I was ready to study for a test I would rethink the notes and write them on the other side. In the textbooks for each class, I would write in the margins and underline text, and I would copy those notes into the notebook, too. That's how I'd get ready for tests.

My fraternity brothers would ask to borrow my notebooks, and I'd let them. Then they'd all get As and I'd get a C. I just didn't know how to take tests. I'd even fuck up multiple choice tests because I'd read the questions incorrectly.

My grades remained pretty good, though. Apart from studying, I was in ROTC, president of my fraternity Sigma Phi Epsilon, and president of the school pep club. I had a couple of side businesses, too. I had always wanted to be a salesman because you didn't have overhead and you got to be the initiator. If you had a store you had to wait for someone to come and see you, but if you were a salesman, you could go to them. I thought it was fun to talk someone into something.

For the homecoming football game, I had the Sig Ep pledges make I's out of pipe cleaners and put them on yellow corsages. I made $2,000 on those in a weekend. Our fraternity was broke, so I gave them the money. The only downside to that was Pop and my mother didn't have money either, and they were paying for my schooling. When I told Pop I'd given the $2,000 to the fraternity, he got upset because he needed that money. So, I went and borrowed money from the student union and gave it to Pop.

Arnie Lefko was my next-door neighbor in Sioux City. His mother and father were wonderful to me, and they had a cleaning supplies company. I asked Arnie if he could get supplies from his parents' company and put them on the train from Sioux City to Iowa City and I would deliver them to the fraternities and sororities. He agreed, and once or twice a month I'd visit with fraternity and sorority house-mothers to get their orders. My friend Pete Castonguay had a Pontiac Tempest convertible, and I paid him two dollars an hour to deliver the orders. The orders were so big that Pete would have to put the top down, and there would be mops and brooms sticking out all over the place. It would be the middle of winter and snowing and he'd be freez-ing his ass off. He'd come back every time cussing me. That little business made me $800 to $900 a year, enough to cover my tuition, room and board, fraternity dues, and more.

For my next business, I made a deal with a dry cleaner to take in laundry from fraternities and sororities at a good price. I'd get a kick-back, and I'd give part of it to each fraternity and sorority.

One day I was in the middle of studying when I got a call from the dry cleaner. "You gotta come over here!" he yelled, and in the back-ground I could hear people screaming and beating on the door.

I got in my car and went over there and people were pissed.

"You have to give them their money back. They're crazy!" the guy shouted. I looked at one of the shirts and the collar was ripped. Another guy's sport coat was wrecked. It was a disaster. So, I gave them back all the money and had to pay a little restitution for the ruined clothes. Looking back on it, it was funny. They were pleased with the corsages and the cleaning supplies, but not the laundry.

While Pop was building his business, he played cards for money. Hell, he always played cards. He played gin and poker at the Empire Club in Sioux City and actually made a living at it. He taught my mother how to play gin, and they played so well that eventually they weren't allowed to play in Sioux City anymore; they had to find games out of town. Pop also got blackballed in Omaha, which is ninety miles away, so they had to go to St. Louis and Kansas City, where the big gin games were at the time. After a good night, they could come home with thousands of dollars. But of course this wasn't a steady income. I still helped out as I could.

One time, Pop and my mother went to play gin in Kansas City, at the Muehlebach Hotel. George E. Muehlebach built the hotel and his dad, George Sr., founded the Muehlebach Brewing Company, which was later bought up by Schlitz. Pop and Mom had to put down $20,000 so the guys putting on the game could make sure they got paid. Pop wrote a check for $20,000, but it wasn't any good. Their plan was that if they lost, they'd excuse themselves, and then run like hell and skip town. Luckily they won.

★★★

I dated a bunch of different girls off and on for a couple of years, but then I started dating the chancellor's daughter for about a year. My mother and Mom Clark, the SigEp house-mother, were conspiring to make sure we didn't get too serious. One day, the girl's mother said she found some contraceptive foam in her daughter's purse and that I had to become Catholic. I told her no and I never saw the girl again. They sent her to Ames, to Iowa State, that very night. It was just as well. Her father was a sweetheart but her mother was crazy. And that's the story of my only steady girlfriend in college.

Pop had just started trading commodities then, and I thought I'd help him out by bringing him a little business. I convinced Mom Clark, who was a doctor's wife and well-to-do, to give Pop $5,000 to trade for her. Now $5,000 was a good bit of money back then. Anyway, he lost every dime. God, I felt terrible, but she never held it against me. About twenty years later I tracked her down and gave her back her $5,000, plus $20,000 more for the time value of the money. She was tickled and said her astrologer told her she was going to come in to some money. We had a good laugh over that.

When I graduated in '64, my mother cried for three days. Every time I looked at her she was crying. She couldn't believe I'd actually made it through four years of college and managed to graduate.

After graduation, I applied for jobs everywhere and didn't get anything. What I really wanted was a job at IBM, which was the hottest company in America at the time. If you worked there, they would give you $100 a month while you were in the military. You also had bragging rights if someone asked, "What are you going to do when you get out of the Army?" I went through their interview process and made it to the very last test. That test had a lot of math on it, and I couldn't even understand the questions, so I knew I didn't do well. When I didn't get the job, I sat in my car and cried. Looking back, it was a good thing.

I had joined ROTC in college because there was a draft at the time. Guys were going to go to war anyway, so I thought I might as well go as an officer. I was supposed to start basic training after graduation, but I thought, why do I want to go back to Sioux City for the summer? I called the draft board on June 1st and asked them if I could start sooner. They told me if I could be at Fort Benning, Georgia, by June 5th, then I could get in. I said, "I'm there."

9

I'M IN THE ARMY NOW

Joining the US Army was absolutely the best thing that ever happened to me. I liked everything about the Army. I still have the opinion that every American should serve in the military. When you're in the military and the commanding officers are spitting in your face as they're yelling at you, you need to get over it. If you have an attitude problem, you'll be doing push-ups for twenty-four hours a day until they get you thinking properly.

On the Fourth of July, 1964, I drove from Fort Benning, Georgia, to Panama City, Florida, with a couple of buddies in my unit. We got to the Holiday Inn and I asked if they had a big double room that we could book for the next three days.

The clerk gave us a look. "You do know this is the Fourth of July, right?" she asked.

"Yes," I said.

"Well, we don't have any room."

"Let me ask you a question," I said. "If the president of the United States were here right now, would you have room for him?"

"Yes, sir!" she answered.

"Well, he's not coming," I told her. "So, I'll take his room." She gave us the room.

My buddies wanted to go out drinking and looking for girls, but I didn't drink then. And remember, nothing good happens after nine o'clock. So they went out and I went to bed. The next thing I knew, guys were banging on the door.

"Dittmer, get out of here. We're bringing the girls in." They told me to take a pillow and blanket and sleep on the walkway outside. So I did.

When the sun came up, I took a walk down to the beach. On the beach were twenty or so college students sitting around a fire and playing guitars. Beautiful women, good-looking guys, and they asked me if I wanted some breakfast. I said I'd love some, thank you. I was talking to this cute girl, and after a while I asked her out to dinner. After dinner we went back to her parents' house and talked and danced on her rooftop. We went out one more night, and then it was time for me to get back to the base. She said she had a girl for me in Columbus, Georgia, which is right by Fort Benning, and told me to call her.

I called this girl as soon as I got back to the base and we made plans to meet up. She was gorgeous! A week later, on Sunday, was the General's Tea. It was a big deal where all the cadets are invited to attend with their wives and girlfriends. I took this beautiful girl as my date. There were 220 guys in my company but only a few of them had dates that night. Before I showed up with this beautiful girl, I might have spoken to three or four of the guys, but after the General's Tea, it was, "Tom, how ya doing?" and "Tom, what's going on?" and "Oh, and by the way, does she have any friends?" I went from obscurity to superstar with that one date. She was great, too. She invited me to her house where there was a party almost every night out by her swimming pool. I can't remember her name, but she was adorable and very nice.

I had been at Fort Benning for four months and was getting ready to graduate, after which I would be assigned to the combat training battalion there. From there, I would be deployed to Vietnam. Before graduation, an officer came by our unit and told us he was going to read off some names and, if our name was on the list, there was a possibility we would be selected to join the 3rd Infantry Regiment, also known as The Old Guard.

My name was on the list, but I didn't know what the 3rd Infantry was. I thought, *Hell, I'm not doing that.* So I left and went to the mess hall. In those days you had to do ten chin-ups before you entered the mess hall. I did my chin-ups, got my tray, sat down, and asked the guy next to me, "So where is the 3rd Infantry, anyway?" He told me it was in Washington, DC. I immediately dropped the tray, ran back out, found the captain, and asked him where I was supposed to be at seven that night.

I didn't eat, but I showered and shaved and put on my madras sport coat, gray slacks, and yellow shirt. I walked into the room and of the forty men there, I was the only guy in civilian clothes. At least they weren't going to ask, "Did he have on the khakis or the fatigues?"

I sat and listened to the spiel and found out that The Old Guard is the oldest active duty regiment in the US Army. It was originally organized as the First American Regiment in 1784. It's the Army's official ceremonial unit and escort to the president. They're responsible for conducting military ceremonies at the White House, the Pentagon, and at national memorials. They keep a twenty-four-hour vigil at The Tomb of the Unknown Soldier, and they are in charge of burials at Arlington National Cemetery. This is a big deal, but what did I know? I was from Iowa. After the spiel and a flag-waving introductory film about The Old Guard, they interviewed me.

"Look," I said, "if you're really the greatest outfit in the world, you need me because I'm going to be the best second lieutenant in the

Army." That got them laughing. When I got back to my room, my roommate Tom Moskas from Worcester, Massachusetts, a big Greek kid, asked me how it went. "I'm in or I'm out," I told him, "but I'm not gray." I was either going to be one of the three guys accepted into The Old Guard or I was going to Vietnam. I had no idea. I was only a second lieutenant and there were some captains in the running.

I was still waiting when I had one day left before reporting for combat training, which meant that in three months I would be in Vietnam. It was 1964, and every three months 90 percent of the guys rotated into Vietnam for a year. Officers in Vietnam were assigned Gurkha bodyguards from a unit called called Mag V, so I had about a 95 percent chance of coming back alive. Eight years later things changed dramatically, and officers probably had about a 95 percent chance of being killed.

A day later, the 3rd Infantry assignment papers came. I was selected. I went to Fort Meyer in Arlington, Virginia, and reported to Delta Company, where I was assigned to Sergeant Smith. My whole life I've been blessed with wonderful people, and Sergeant Smith was one of them. He was an E-5, meaning three stripes up and two stripes down. He was from the South, a "dos and don'ts" kind of guy with missing teeth. He spent five years in combat in Korea and Vietnam. He was a little shell-shocked and definitely not a parade soldier. I was a parade soldier. In two weeks we'd have to go into the field for a month to compete in the annual battalion war games. He knew how to play. I wasn't the guy; Sergeant Smith was the guy.

"Sergeant Smith," I said to him, "you know that I'm barely a second lieutenant."

"Yes, sir," he said.

"That means I can use all the help I can get."

"Lieutenant," he said, "I'll take care of you and you're going to have fun. You're going to win the battalion games and I'm going to show you how."

These war games were held at Fort A.P. Hill near Bowling Green, Virginia. There were six companies and four platoons in each company competing. Every night in our tent, I'd get the maps out and tell Sergeant Smith what we were supposed to do the next day and then ask him how to do it. He'd run down what we should do, and that's exactly what we would do. When you're a schmuck from Sioux City and you're doing combat exercises with a combat sergeant, you listen to him.

We won the games. No one could believe it and guys in the company were asking, "Who is this guy?" I was competing against first lieutenants and guys with a lot more experience than I had, and I had only been there for thirty days. The reason we won was Sergeant Smith.

Four months later I was invited to join the Delta Company Honor Guard, and that was a big deal. I even had a key to Arlington Cemetery. We had the responsibility of guarding The Tomb of the Unknown Soldier, and when a soldier died in Vietnam and came home to be buried in Arlington, we escorted him to his final resting place in the Gardens of Stone. When there was a state funeral at the Rotunda, the Honor Guard pulled the duty. We also guarded the Kennedy gravesite.

I was also the officer in charge of the US Army Drill Team, an elite precision drill platoon that performed for military, government, and civilian organizations. We were invited to perform on *The Ed Sullivan Show*. I was on for five minutes.

Another time we were doing an exhibition, and one of the soldiers misthrew his weapon. The bayonet pierced right through the hand of the guy who was supposed to catch it. He pulled it out, re-shouldered the gun, and kept marching. When it was over and we were off the field, he passed out and was rushed directly to the hospital, but by God he didn't miss a step on that parade. He was okay, by the way—really lucky. Serving in the Honor Guard was a great job and a great honor.

10

POP GOES INTO COMMODITIES

When I went into the Army in '64, Pop went into the commodities business with Gil Miller, who ran a clearinghouse in Chicago. Gil was an old egg guy who gave up the egg business and went into commodities, trading egg futures on the Chicago Mercantile Exchange, also called the Merc. Since Pop had been in the egg-breaking business and knew a lot of people, he started out trading egg futures. At the time the Merc was low rent compared to the Board of Trade. The Merc was for the Jews and the Board of Trade was for the Irish. In the end, the Irish went out of business and the Jews bought them out. Between the commodities business and playing gin rummy, Pop managed to make a modest income, but his business didn't really take off until about '66, which was when I left the Army.

In November of '64, the Merc introduced futures contracts on live cattle, and Pop started trading in those, too. It was a new thing, and it was like the Wild West. People were trading like crazy.

Pop and my mother went to work every morning in the stockyards at the Sioux City Livestock Exchange. He sat on an orange crate taking orders, next to Mother who stood by a big chalkboard. Mother would watch the ticker tape, which transmitted stock prices over the telegraph lines, and she'd write the quotes on the chalkboard for the cattlemen who walked by. Later on, Pop built an office out of sawed lumber in the livestock exchange lobby, and he had a big glass window so everyone could see his chalkboard.

Once there was this loudmouth guy who decided to razz my mother while she was working.

"Why don't you buy me some of those cattle?" asked the loudmouth.

"Ray," my mother said without even looking at the guy, "buy that guy three hundred cattle futures."

"No! No, no," the guy yelled.

"No?" said my mother. "Well, to me three hundred futures is some." She was ornerier than hell.

During the day, Pop and Mother would work until one o'clock and then go home to have lunch. That's when Pop would invite all of his friends over to play cards until finally my mother had enough. "Ray, this is like a pool hall. Everyone is smoking, you're playing cards. I'm about to cook dinner, and then you're going to want them to stay for dinner. Now come on!"

Pop toned it down a little bit after that. He even quit smoking cold turkey. But he still played cards every day.

11

FRANNIE

In early 1964, I met Frances "Frannie" Ronshausen in Arlington.
Once a quarter, the general of the military district of Washington,
who was stationed in Fort Meyer, would invite all the new officers to
his house for dinner. The general's daughter was one of Frannie's
roommates, and they were invited, too. The first time I saw Frannie
coming down the stairs at the general's house, I thought, *Well, I like
that.* I managed to get across the room to talk to her.

"Would you like to go for a walk?" I asked her.

It had just snowed and she looked at me like, "What?"

"It just snowed," I said. "Don't you want to walk in the snow?"

"No," she said.

"Okay, okay," I said. "I'll give you another chance. How about some
hot apple pie à la mode at the Key Bridge Marriott?"

"What?" she asked.

"Key Bridge Marriott, hot apple pie à la mode. You can't go wrong."

I think the only reason she went with me was because she was curi-
ous about what kind of fruitcake I was. She had her car with her, so I

met her at the Marriott and we had pie and talked. I then followed her home and got out and gave her a little kiss.

"I don't kiss on the first date," she said.

"You've got a perfect record then," I said, "because that wasn't a kiss." I walked away thinking she was kind of a bitch. I got home and my roommates Watson, Sylvester, Holland, and Nye were sitting in the kitchen drinking beer.

I told them, "I'm not taking her out again. She wouldn't even kiss me." But a few days later, I was thinking about giving her a call.

Frannie was born in Texas and graduated from the University of Texas at Austin. After college she went to secretarial school because her mother told her that she either had to become a secretary or a nurse, and she didn't want to be a nurse. She applied for a job with Texas Senator Ralph Yarborough and was hired into the typing pool. By the time I met her she had become his private secretary. Frannie shared an apartment with eight roommates. It was right on D Street, close enough for her to walk to the office.

Smilin' Ralph, as they called him, was head of the progressive wing of the Democratic Party and the only senator to vote for all the civil rights bills from 1957 to 1970. When President Kennedy was assassinated, Senator Yarborough was sitting in the second car of the motorcade with Vice President Johnson and Lady Bird. He was quite a character and had a reputation for giving fiery speeches. His campaign slogan was "Let's put the jam on the lower shelf so the little people can reach it."

On the Tuesday following our apple pie à la mode date when I decided not to call her again, I called and asked her to dinner for Saturday night. I told her I thought we'd go to the Knife and Fork Club, which was a fancy place I couldn't afford. She said she'd love to go. My mother always told me, "Go out once right and not four times half assed." This date with Frannie was going to be "once right."

Frannie's mother had always told her if she was asked to a fancy restaurant, then go.

We were sitting in the bar at the Knife and Fork Club waiting for our table. I was twenty-three years old and had never had a drink in my life. I asked Frannie if she'd like a drink and she ordered a gin martini. "Make it two," I told the bartender, because I had no idea what to order.

We had our drinks and soon our table was ready. We started down the stairs to the dining room, and, God it seemed like a lot of stairs. I was weaving and hanging onto the banister, thinking, *Jesus Christ, I can hardly stand up.* We finally got to our table and we ordered some red wine. They brought it sort of propped in an oblong wicker basket and instead of holding it from the sides to pour it, I picked it up by the handle. Wine spilled all over the table, and all over Frannie.

"What are you doing?" asked Frannie, not happy. "My dress!"

The waiter soon passed by, and he was horrified because he thought one of the servers did it.

"No," I said. "I did it."

"I'm sorry," I said to Frannie. "I've never had a drink before."

She went from hostile to sweet in an instant. And when we finished dinner she invited me back to her apartment. I was thinking that maybe I'd get a kiss. I liked Frannie a lot, and we started going steady. She was cute, funny, smart, tall, and I loved her Southern drawl.

Meanwhile, Pop was struggling in the commodities business and, at one point, I'd borrowed $3,000 from the Army Credit Union to help him out. This time I convinced Frannie to go in with me on a trading venture with him. She put up $750 and I put up $250, and we became partners trading pork bellies. I sent the money off to Pop, and we lost the whole $1,000.

Frannie asked how our investment was doing, and I told her it was good, no problem. But then Pop and Mother came to visit us in

Washington. We were at dinner one night and Pop said to Frannie, "I'm awful sorry about your money."

"What?" Frannie said. "Tom said we were doing just fine."

"Oh, no," Pop said. "We lost it all."

Frannie was mad, really mad. "You're a shyster!" she shouted at me. Pop never forgave her for that. She had questioned my honor and my integrity. Of course, I did lie to her and I did lose her money. My mother got over it because she knew that our relationship was going somewhere, and that alienating Frannie would be a mistake.

Frannie, still mad at me, called a week later and told me that she had to go to a party and needed a date. "Just meet me there," she said, "and don't be an asshole. Then, after the party, you go your way and I'll go mine."

"Fine," I said. I went to meet her at some senator's party and, by the way, I wasn't drinking anymore. We stayed at the party for a while and then left. I walked one way down the sidewalk and she walked the other. Then I stopped and looked back at her, and she had stopped to look back at me, too. I said, "You want to get a cup of coffee?"

"Yes," she said. Frannie could act like a hard-ass, but at the end of the day she really wasn't.

We got back together and then Frannie went off to Europe for the summer. After I lost her money, she'd had to sell her Volkswagen Beetle for $1,000 to be able to afford the trip. She wrote me every day while she was away. I wrote to her, too, but I hadn't worked out the lead time, and not a single one of my letters got to her.

When it was time for Frannie to come back to the States, she sent me a message: "I'm coming into Dulles at two o'clock if you want to pick me up. Otherwise, I understand."

I went to my captain and said, "Captain, I've got to get off. I have to go to the airport."

"I can let you go at one thirty," he said.

"But I have to shower and change," I said.

"No, one thirty is the earliest you can get out of here. Just go in your fatigues."

It was summer and I'd been working. I was sweating and in a panic about not making it to the airport on time. I was running and out of breath and worried sick when I got there, but there she was, standing in the middle of the terminal with her back to me. I could see that she'd lost weight, probably because she couldn't afford to eat much on her trip. I looked at her and I thought when I touched her, I'd be able to tell if this was it, if she was the one. If she was crazy about me, I'd know it. She was standing there with her two suitcases, and then she put them down to look around and see if I was there. I walked up behind her, spun her around, gave her a kiss, and she just melted into me. Then I knew.

12

THE WHITE HOUSE

I'd seen this guy around The Old Guard who had a presidential seal on his jacket. I asked someone who he was and was told that he was a White House social aide.

"How do you get to be one of those?" I asked.

"They have to ask you," the guy told me.

"Look," I told him. "I don't have time for that. How do you get to be one?"

"If you know senators and congressmen, that'll help."

Fortunately, there was both a senator and a congressman from Sioux City, and I had dated both of their daughters in high school. They were wonderful gentlemen. I called up each one.

"I'd like to become a White House social aide," I said. "Can you help me?"

Both of them said they'd be delighted to help me. It only took three weeks or so before I got a call from the White House saying they were sending a car to pick me up for an interview with Bess Abell, who was President Johnson's Social Secretary. I was waiting for her outside her office on the South Portico, and I heard her on the phone. She was cussing up a blue streak. I mean, things came out of her mouth I'd never heard before.

"Second lieutenant, come in here."

I went into her office.

"Do you dance?" she asked.

"Yes ma'am," I said.

"Do you like girls?"

"Yes ma'am."

That was the end of the interview. The limousine dropped me back at Fort Meyer, and the colonel, the battalion commander, called me in.

"Lieutenant, I saw you get into a White House limousine, and while I'm not positive what you were up to, I've got a pretty good idea, so I'm just going to tell you what the rules are around here. We do not want any of our officers to become White House social aides."

I guess he thought the nighttime duties of a social aide might interfere with the daytime duties of a 3rd Infantryman.

"Is that clear?" the colonel barked.

"Yes, sir."

"Am I clear?"

"You're absolutely clear, sir."

I left the colonel and immediately got on the phone with the senator and congressman.

"Listen, can you push these guys faster because the colonel is pissed at me," I tell them.

I was twenty-four years old and of course they had to do a background check on me. Being from Sioux City, there wasn't much background. They did call my neighbors, though, and went to talk with them.

Not long after that the limousine came and took me to the White House again. I'd been chosen to become a White House social aide. Got the seal on my jacket and everything.

When I got back to the battalion, the first sergeant found me. "The colonel is looking for you," he said.

I found my captain and we went into the colonel's office.

"Lieutenant," the colonel asked, "where was I not clear?"

"Sir, you were very clear."

"And yet," he said, "you've gone ahead and become a White House social aide in spite of my directive."

"Yes, sir," I said.

"And the reason?"

"Sir, there is no excuse," I said.

He's quiet for a moment. "Well . . . congratulations."

That's standard military. Blow something up and then say, "Ah, it's okay." I think it was actually good for the colonel to have his officers in the White House because it was considered an honor.

My job as a social aide was to attend state functions, usher people in, talk to them, and introduce them around. The aides were each assigned a section of the room and told which guests they were to meet. I'd take the guests to my corner of the room, introduce everyone, dance with the ladies, and usher them all into the dining room. When we finished for the night, all the aides would go the Navy mess to have dinner, which was always great.

I continued serving with the 3rd Infantry during the day, conducting burials at Arlington, guarding The Tomb of the Unknown Soldier and the Kennedy grave, and providing state funeral escorts. So, I essentially had a day job and a night job. I'd work anywhere from one to five nights a week, and I was still dating Frannie. Talk about burning your candle at both ends.

Every company in the US military selects an Officer of the Day every day, and this officer is on call through the night. If there's a problem, or someone gets in trouble, the Officer of the Day gets the call. When I was selected to be the Officer of the Day, I would go and check on both the tomb and the cemetery at night. Sometimes I would take Frannie with me and we'd sit on the steps of the Custis-Lee Mansion that overlooks 250,000 military gravesites, the National Mall, and the Potomac River. There was something really beautiful about that view.

Charlie Beasley, a Navy guy, was skipper of the USS *Sequoia*, the presidential yacht. Built in 1925, the vessel was 105 feet long, had a wooden hull, and was covered in presidential seals. It was used by every president, from Herbert Hoover to Jimmy Carter, until Carter sold it in 1977. An elevator had been installed in the yacht for FDR, but Johnson had it replaced by a bar. LBJ also used to watch movies on the top deck using the smokestack for a screen.

After a state dinner, the aides, all sixteen of us—four from each branch of the service—would frequently go out in the USS *Sequoia*, and we'd eat dinner at its original old mahogany dining table, which could seat as many as twenty-two.

One night after leaving the White House, I went to pick up Frannie and bring her to the boat. When she came aboard, all the guys, still in their dress uniforms, stood up holding glasses of champagne. "Lovey," I said to Frannie, "will you marry me?" She was so surprised she didn't know what to do, but luckily for me she said yes. Everybody cheered, we had dinner, and I took Frannie home. The next day I went back to work. I couldn't afford an engagement ring, and as a matter fact, Frannie ended up buying our wedding rings.

On Labor Day in '65, all the aides decided we were going to take our girlfriends out for a moonlight sail on the *Sequoia*. We were out, having fun. When we got back at one in the morning, Marvin Watson, a former Marine who had served in World War II, confronted me. Watson's official title was White House Appointments Secretary, but he was basically chief of staff. He later wrote a book titled *Chief of Staff* about his years with President Johnson.

That night, Watson wasn't very happy with us.

"Dittmer?" Watson said to me. "Lieutenant?"

"Yes, sir."

"We want you at the South Portico at zero seven hundred hours."

The aides all arrived at the South Portico at the appointed time, and we were all looking at each other thinking, *Shit.* We figured it had to do with the boat. When Watson showed up, he informed us President Johnson had called the night before and wanted to take some people out on the boat for an evening cruise. And there we were with the boat. Not good.

Watson said, "This happens again and you assholes will be in Vietnam before sunset. Is that clear?"

Yes, that was as clear as crystal.

We were at the White House two weeks later when I observed the president dancing with Princess Lee Radziwill, Jacqueline Kennedy's sister. One of the aides at the time was this handsome colonel, Colonel White—I mean movie star handsome and an ace Navy pilot with the cocky attitude to match. He couldn't stand LBJ. Colonel White walked up to LBJ and Princess Radziwill and tapped the President on the shoulder. I couldn't believe what was happening.

"Excuse me, Mr. President," Colonel White said, "may I cut in, please?" There wasn't a White House social aide breathing. This guy was daring to cut in on the president of the United States at a dance in his own house. *Oh, fuck,* I was thinking. *We'll be in Vietnam by morning!*

Once again, at 0700 at the South Portico, Marvin Watson stood there glaring at us. "You don't ever cut in on the president! Ever! Is that understood?"

It was understood.

LBJ spoke to me only once during my time as an aide. One day I was assigned to his detail and my job was to welcome in and then escort the Texas Teachers Union group upstairs. Otherwise, I was supposed to hover nearby the president in case he needed something while also staying out of his way.

"Lieutenant," Watson instructed me, "I want you to go down to the East Portico and let the teachers in. Protect yourself first, the White House second."

Teachers Union? Protect myself? Why?

I went down to the East Portico and opened the door. There were at least five hundred people there, and they were like a mob storming the gates. As they pushed past me, they tried to pull off my aiguillettes, my nameplate, everything, anything. They wanted souvenirs. I got them upstairs and, before I knew it, there wasn't an ashtray left in the room. They even took the cocktail forks. It was unbelievable. So the president was meeting with the Texas Teachers Union while they were pillaging the White House.

Later in the day, things had calmed down, and I was hovering near the president in case he needed me. I took my gloves off, picked up a tortilla chip, and put it in my mouth. Just as I did that, President Johnson turned to me and said, "Lieutenant, take Mr. and Mrs. So-and-So up to the Lincoln Bedroom." I quickly swallowed the chip and as I was walking away, he said, "Lieutenant, you're here to work, not to eat." That's the only time he ever talked to me.

During my time as a social aide, the president's daughter, Lynda Bird, dated my roommate at Fort Meyer, John Betar, and Frannie and I would go out with them occasionally. Later in life I would get to know both Lynda and President Johnson's younger daughter, Luci, and was fond of them both.

13

I FIND WHERE I BELONG

I finished my stint in the Army in June 1966. That same month, President Johnson granted a full pardon to Pop. I've been asked if my being a White House social aide had anything to do with the pardon. I don't know, but I did what I could. I talked to senators and congressmen. I got names of people in Washington to call to tell me what steps to take. I'd tell Pop, and he would tell his lawyer, and they would do what they could from their end as well. His case had been a federal offense, which meant he wasn't eligible to vote. Being a squeaky wheel in Washington probably didn't hurt, but I was only a twenty-four-year-old second lieutenant making $340 a month. The White House gardener was higher up in the food chain than I was, but I think I helped.

By the time I got out of the service, Pop was on the rise. He and Mom built a big house in Country Club, which was the fancy area of Sioux City. It sat on four or five acres and was complemented by a swimming pool, guesthouse, and two tennis courts.

I had planned on joining Pop in the commodities business while I was still in the Army. My job-hunting experience after college had me believing that I couldn't get a job anywhere else. It didn't occur to me that my military experience or my selection for those elite Army units was a plus in terms of getting hired. I just didn't have much confidence in that area, and deep down I knew that I wanted to work for myself.

Frannie and I were engaged, but she was still working in DC when I moved to Chicago. I rented a wonderful brownstone for $160 a month at 1450 North Dearborn Street, which was a great location. Today the location is still great and that same place would rent for around $3,000 a month. It had a big living room, high ceilings, a huge bedroom, a backyard, and a one-car garage. The kitchen was the size of a coffee table, which was perfect for Frannie because she didn't cook.

In order for me to learn the commodities business, Pop got me a job with his old friend and mentor, Gil Miller. I made $82 a week as a runner on the floor of the Chicago Mercantile Exchange, and I was glad to get it. After paying for rent and other expenses, I had enough money left over for one meal a day. I went from 185 pounds to 155 in four months.

I loved the floor of the Merc from the minute I walked onto it. I knew this was it; I was exactly where I belonged. There were thousands of guys on the floor, smoking, screaming, yelling, and trading. The energy in the room was amazing. I could walk in there and the market would be doing nothing and everyone would be standing around. Then I'd feel something. I'd feel the energy building and suddenly the market would erupt, up or down. Everybody would start screaming and yelling, pushing and shoving. It was incredible, it was exciting, and it was a ball. Guys would have heart attacks in there and traders would just step over them. An employee who was not trading would take the guy by the feet and drag him out. No one even slowed down.

In those days, runners would take the order on the phone and then run into the pit and give it to the guys who filled the orders. The guys who filled the orders made $1.50 an order, and they could make one to two million dollars a year back then. Blackboards lined a balcony above the pits. Guys with chalk would have phones stuck to their ears, and they'd be marking stuff on the blackboards like crazy. You had your card and pencil in your hand and you had to call out your buy or sell and hold your hand straight up; it was so crowded that if you held your hand at an angle, you'd risk poking someone's eye out. To do business on the floor, you had to have a membership, which in 1966 cost $25,000.

I didn't have a membership and couldn't afford one, but in September I started doing a little business on the floor on the sly and got caught. They threw me off the floor, and I was banished upstairs to Gil's office. I had a tiny cubicle up there with a phone, a map of the Midwest, and one of those page-a-day calendars. Every day, Herb Turmin, an old egg trader, would walk by, and finally after about a week he said, "You don't have any idea what to do, do you?"

"Not a clue," I told him.

Herb took me into his office and laid out a map. "You're right here," he said, pointing to Chicago. He took out his compass and drew a fifty-mile radius from the center of Chicago, and then he drew another circle at a hundred miles, and then at a hundred fifty miles. "You start in the first circle," he said. "You write down every little farm town in that circle, and you go get the Yellow Pages and look up every feed and fertilizer dealer and every cattle rancher in those towns."

"Where do I do that?" I asked.

He pointed across the street and said, "There's the headquarters for AT&T. On the third floor is every Yellow Pages in the country. That's where you go."

So, I went across the street to AT&T, found the Yellow Pages, and started calling. And that's how I built the business. I called all the businesses within the three circles. I would tell them, "I have an idea. I'm bullish on cattle or I'm bearish on this." It was cold calling; I hated it but I had to do it.

14

FRANNIE AND I GET MARRIED

Frannie quit her job in DC and in October 1966, we went to Texas to get married. We had a small ceremony in a church in Port Arthur, where Frannie was from. I had my old college roommate Corky Kress and my mother and Pop with me, and that was it. The whole wedding cost $150, and the reception was held at Frannie's aunt's house where we had watermelon, punch, and cake.

Right after the reception, Frannie and I caught a commuter plane to Houston, where we checked into the Shamrock Hotel, which was like the Ritz of Houston. I had been there before and the guy who ran it was from Iowa. He gave us the best room he had for $100. It was an eight-room suite, and it was quite a night.

The next morning, we got ready to go to Mexico City for our honeymoon. I went to get us a taxi, but there are no taxis in Houston like there are in Chicago and New York, so I had to go down the street to find one, and it made us late. We were booked on Pan Am Flight #1 to Mexico City, leaving at 9:00 but we didn't arrive at the airport until

8:55. Frannie went to the ticket counter and I got the bags. I heard the agent say that our flight was leaving from Gate 1.

"You're too late," the agent said to Frannie.

"The gate is right there," I said. "I can see it. The walkway is still up."

"It's still too late," he said.

I didn't care. We were going. I was so mad thinking about how this was my first day in charge and I'd already managed to fuck it up. I was gonna kill that little motherfucker. I walked to the automatic glass doors leading to the gate, but they didn't open fast enough and I walked right through them. Shards of glass flew everywhere! My hands and face got all cut up and I was covered in glass.

The Texas Rangers quickly arrived on the scene and they were all over me. I was bleeding everywhere, so they took me into the bathroom. "Oh, take care of him, take care of him!" Frannie shouted.

"Oh, we'll take care of him all right," one of the Rangers snapped back. Then they took me to the hospital where the doctors taped me up and gave me a few stitches. I was lucky not to have been more seriously injured, and I'm sure if the same thing happened today, I'd be arrested.

We went back to the airport, but there were no more direct flights to Mexico City that day so we had to book one that connected in San Antonio. My Aunt Irene once teased Frannie, saying, "He can't read, can't write, and can't talk. Why are you marrying him?" Frannie was probably wondering the same thing at this time. Eventually we landed in San Antonio and went to the St. Anthony Hotel, where we were met by a group of Frannie's college friends who were going to have dinner with us. I was standing outside the hotel and her friends were looking at me like "Who is this guy with the bandages all over him?" But after dinner we went back to the airport and got on the plane bound for Mexico City.

When we landed in Mexico City, we learned that another plane had crashed on the runway. When we finally got to our fancy hotel, we learned that our room wasn't ready and it wouldn't be for some time because the people who were supposed to take the airplane that crashed couldn't leave and were staying at the hotel. The desk clerk made a reservation for us at another hotel. It was about three in the morning by this point, and we took a taxi to the next hotel. Not only was the place a dump, but the only room they had was one with twin beds. Oh, great.

The next morning we got up, had some coffee, went on a little tour, ate lunch, and then both of us were immediately stricken with Montezuma's revenge. We had planned to go to Acapulco the next day, but I happened to notice Frannie's checkbook sitting out on the table. Pop had given me $1,000 to buy the plane tickets, and Frannie was going to pay for some of the other expenses. She was supposed to have $4,000 in her account, but as I was looking at her checkbook I saw a zero balance.

"No, no," she insisted. "I have $4,000."

"Well, when I add up the numbers it comes to zero," I said. "What do you get?"

She looked. "Oh! We don't have any money!" So not only were we stuck in a shitty hotel on our honeymoon, sick as dogs, we were also broke.

We went back to the airport and flew back to Houston and then to Port Arthur, where we spent the rest of our honeymoon at her parents' house. When her parents ventured into the backyard, I said to Frannie, "Honey, come on, let's—"

"No, no, they'll hear!" she told me.

"They think we're having sex anyway."

"No, they don't," Frannie says, horrified at the thought.

Needless to say, it was the worst honeymoon ever.

I was looking forward to getting back to Chicago, but before we got married, I had to promise Frannie that we would move back to Houston as soon as possible. She didn't want to live in the North because she hated the North. You know, Yankees. We landed in Chicago after the honeymoon and Frannie started crying.

"Frannie, what are you crying about?" I said.

"I'll never see my parents again. We're so poor," she wailed. "There are probably factories on the main street of Chicago."

I didn't really know what to say, but I was thinking I needed this like a hole in the head. "No," I said, "it's actually pretty nice." We got to the apartment and it was furnished with a king-size bed, an unfinished dresser from Sears, and a clock radio. That was it. Frannie started crying again. She went into the bathroom crying, came out crying, and got into bed—still crying.

While we were engaged, Frannie had said to me that she wanted to make me breakfast every morning before I went to work. "Gee, that would be great," I told her. So the first morning after we got back to Chicago, I got up and woke up Frannie. "Honey, do you want to make me breakfast?" I asked.

"Oh, what time is it?"

"5:30."

"5:30?! What are you doing?" she asked like I was crazy.

"I'm going to work."

"5:30?!"

She was clearly irritated but got out of bed anyway. She went into the kitchen and reached into the cupboard. *Bam*, she slammed the cereal box on the counter and cornflakes flew everywhere. Then she slammed the milk down—*bam*—and milk spilled everywhere. Then she slammed the bowl down, *bam*. "Breakfast. Okay?"

"Do me a favor," I said. "Don't make breakfast anymore." That was the last time Frannie ever made breakfast. I thought it was funny later, but at the time I thought, *Oh, God, this is my partner?* And she cried constantly. I mean, all the time.

The only coat Frannie had when she first moved to Chicago was a cloth coat. To get to work she had to catch the bus on North Avenue and Lake Shore Drive, which becomes Michigan Avenue as it moves south. The wind coming off of Lake Michigan had to be about twenty or thirty knots in the winter, and the temperature was maybe five above zero on a "warm" day. She'd come home with icicles hanging off of her. "We have to get you a wool coat," I told her. She got a wool coat and life got a little bit better after that.

I would drive to little towns and give talks about commodities. Frannie would help me write a market letter and mail it out to my customer list. I still wasn't making much money, only around $1,000 to $2,000 a month in commissions. Frannie, meanwhile, had gotten a job making $26,000 a year working as a sort of administrative editor for the books division of IBM. That was a lot of money in 1966, and she supported us financially while we both worked to build our commodities business.

15

EARLY LIFE IN CHICAGO

The Chicago Union Stockyards were 475 acres full of hogs, cattle, and other livestock that had been shipped from all over the country. It had been a major industrial hub in Chicago for more than a century. It was where people bought and sold livestock, corn, and soybean meal as feed. These were the people I wanted to do business with.

Every winter there was a big expo-type event. I got a crappy booth, which Gil Miller bought for $150. It was by the back door, practically outside, and I froze my ass off. I got free brochures from the Exchange, and in five days, saying the same things I'd been saying on the phone, I walked out of there with $250,000 in checks from guys who wanted to trade with me. That's when I really began.

Our social life started to pick up, too. Frannie had gone to school with Clare Kobluk, who was married to Mike Kobluk, one of the original members of the Chad Mitchell Trio. Mike, William Chadbourne "Chad" Mitchell, and Mike Pugh had all been in the glee club together at Gonzaga University in Spokane, Washington, where they formed their famous trio in the late 1950s. In 1967 Clare and Mike were in DC while the trio was singing at the Cellar Door. Clare called Frannie and said, "Why don't you and Tom come to Washington? We have this new singer, John Deutschendorf." That was before he changed his name to John Denver.

Coincidentally, Mike and Clare, John and his wife, Annie, and Frannie and I had moved to Chicago around the same time. None of us really knew anybody in Chicago, so on Friday nights we'd all get together. John would get out his guitar and we'd say, "John, put away the fucking guitar, we want to talk."

The first Thanksgiving that Frannie cooked—or tried to cook— was for Mike and Clare, and John and Annie. As I was carving into the turkey, I noticed something odd. I reached into the carcass and pulled out the plastic package of giblets. Frannie had baked them into the turkey. Like I said, she wasn't much of a cook. After dinner, John and I went to Butch McGuire's, a bar on Division Street that's become a legend since then and is still there. Since it was Thanksgiving, the place was quiet. We were playing tabletop shuffleboard and talking about life and what we wanted out of it. John was telling me how he was going to be one of the biggest songwriters ever. I told him how I was going to build a clearinghouse and we were going to make all this money. That was our Thanksgiving together and, as it turned out, both of our dreams came true.

Frannie and I saw John and Annie over the years, but after they divorced we only saw her, and we saw her a lot. The last time we saw John was when we took all the kids to see a rocket launch at Cape Canaveral. When John died, Annie inherited all of his royalty rights. She told us he made more money after he died on those John Denver Greatest Hits albums than he did with all his years of live entertaining.

By the end of '67, I had made over $50,000, so things were definitely looking up. I was still working upstairs in Gil's office, and they were taking a 50 percent cut of everything I made. I was still making cold calls and sending out my market letters on my own nickel. The next year I made over $200,000. I went home and told Frannie, "Honey, good news. We can move back to Houston."

"What?" Frannie asked.

"We're moving back to Houston, like you made me promise you we would."

"Are you crazy?" she said. "Chicago is fabulous. Why would anybody want to move to Houston?!"

This was the same woman who cried for the first year she was in Chicago, but she had grown to love it. We had made friends with at least a hundred other couples. It's a friendly town because everybody comes there from someplace else and they all want to meet somebody. But we never socialized with my friends from work because Frannie thought everybody in the commodities business were sleazeballs, and she didn't want them around. And she was kind of right. She had joined the Travelers Aid Society, which had been around since the late 1800s, organized to help immigrants, the unemployed, and servicemen. They held fund-raisers, meetings, and parties three or four times a year.

"Honey, I don't want to go to Travelers Aid," I told Frannie one night.

"We're going," she said, so of course we went.

I walked in and I'd never seen that many gorgeous women all in one place before. Later, I was in the bathroom and I asked the guy next to me, "Is it always this way? Are there always so many beautiful women?"

"I never miss one," the guy said.

"I'm with him," said the guy on the other side of me. "This is the best."

We never missed another one either.

From Travelers Aid we just kept making more and more friends. Almost everyone on our street was from someplace else. It seemed like everyone from Iowa, Indiana, Wisconsin, and all of those little towns I visited for work wanted to move to Chicago.

I met AW Moursund through a cattle buyer from Sioux City who told me AW was in Texas and wanted to trade commodities. I knew about AW because he was a big buddy of LBJ and a trustee of his estate when he was president. And, funnily enough, AW and LBJ looked near 'bout like twins. They even sounded alike. So, AW came up to Chicago and I hustled him. He wanted to see how the Exchange worked, so I took him to the egg pit. I was twenty-six years old and I finally had a membership, but I was still a rookie with an itty-bitty account. So I walked into the pit and signaled—with a combination of sign language and shouting—that I wanted to buy five egg contracts. The guy taking the orders yelled at me, "Nah, take fifty."

Now, I had Mr. Big Texas standing there, and I was too proud to wuss out and say, "But I only want five." Before I knew it, two other guys sold me fifty contracts each, just by sheer bullying. Now I only had maybe $5,000 in my account at the time, yet suddenly I was on the hook for about $150,000 worth of eggs. If Moursund hasn't been standing there, I wouldn't have done it, but I had to be macho. The second he left I ran to Gil and told him about the fix I was in.

Right at that minute, a fight broke out in the pit and everybody was yelling. I ran over and saw that there was a limit-up bid, which means the price can't go up any higher in that trading session. So I ran back to Gil and asked him if I could keep the contracts until the next day, which I did. Now I was making some real money. I asked Gil if I could keep 'em another day, and he agreed. And on that next day, I sold. I made over $200,000, more money than I'd ever made in my entire life. That's almost $1.5 million in today's dollars. And it was all because of my dumbass mistake! I was just in the right place at the right time. Everybody has a moment, and that was mine.

AW and I later bought ranches and did business together, but shortly after my big adventure in the egg pit, he called me. "By gawd, Tom," he started out in his Texas drawl. "I have a friend in Chicago you should know. His name is Henry Crown. I'm going to call him and have him ask you to lunch."

I was in the same building as Henry Crown, and it was called the Crown Building. Henry calls me. "Come up for lunch, one o'clock tomorrow," he said.

Most people have no idea what this man accomplished. His parents were Jewish immigrants from Lithuania, and they were sweatshop workers who raised seven kids. Henry had an eighth grade education. He owned huge interests in General Dynamics and Aspen Ski Corporation and he had great kids and died a billionaire. I went up to see him, and we didn't go to any fancy executive dining room. We ate sandwiches at his desk. This was one of the wealthiest men in Chicago and I was an absolute nobody, but there I was, having a sandwich with Henry Crown at his desk. That was Henry, and that was Chicago.

16

REFCO

In October 1969, Pop and I officially formed our partnership, Ray E. Friedman & Co., or Refco). Pop was still living in Sioux City, but we opened our office in the Chicago Mercantile Exchange building. I was twenty-eight years old and Pop was in his fifties. He owned 75 percent of the company and I owned 25 percent. We made money from day one because we already had our own business. He was making about $15 million a year in commissions, while I was making about $5 million. Pop told me he would pay me a salary, but if he did, I couldn't trade. I told him, "I'm trading!" So I never made a salary. I haven't made a salary in thirty years. Frannie quit her job that same year and started working in the company along with Rose Papas, who was our office manager and bookkeeper.

We were buying and selling commodities over the telephone using the ticker tape. We were considered wild risk-takers because we were trading on our own in the meat and grain pits and at the same time handling customer accounts. We became popular with the traders because we knew what they were dealing with. More than once I was called a bad-boy gunslinger because I could make or lose millions of dollars in a week. It was Pop who gave me all the opportunities, and without him it never would have happened for me.

In '71 President Nixon "closed the gold window" and changed life for a lot of people in the world by devaluing the US dollar, which had been fixed relative to gold for almost thirty years. Prior to '71, foreign central banks could trade in their dollars for gold, and the fear was that US gold reserves were being placed at risk because of the growing accumulation of dollars abroad. Nixon and his advisors decided that closing the gold window would allow foreign currencies to fluctuate and likely strengthen against the dollar. A weaker dollar would help US exports, which would help the US economy. Part of it was political, as Nixon wanted to run for reelection. Another part of it was because Treasury Secretary John Connally didn't want a run on US gold reserves or to be put in a position to have to deny foreign requests for US gold. And although the weaker dollar did boost exports, the dollar plunged by about a third in value, inflation skyrocketed, interest rates soared, and American manufacturing began its great decline. With the number of dollars no longer fixed to the amount of gold reserves, the government could print as much money as it liked. And that, in a nutshell, is what got us in the mess and the debt we're in today.

Gold in the '70s was valued at $35 an ounce. At this writing in 2018, it's closer to $1,300 an ounce. You can see what has happened to your dollar since 1971. Look at housing. Before 1971, people didn't look at their houses as an asset class. The furnace would break, the hot water heater would break, the roof leaked, something was always wrong with it. By the '80s, though, that same house was worth many times more than what they paid for it. If you look at a corn-trading chart from 1871 to 1971, you'll see that it is relatively flat. Corn traded from $1 to $1.20. Soybeans traded from $2.50 to $3. That's how it was for a hundred years. But then, in 1973, corn went to $4 and soybeans to $12. When you close the gold window, the dollar goes down and prices go up. What's your next hard asset? It is your house and commodities. I was in commodities. Refco was in commodities. Business went through the roof, and that made the business.

17

A FAMILY MAN

I was really happy when Frannie got pregnant. When we got married, my mother had told us, "I'm not counting from the day you get married. Any day now is fine for my grandchild. I hope it's next week." Five years later, Frannie got pregnant. The day she went into labor was just like in the movies. She had packed her suitcase, and early one morning, her water broke.

"I think we should go to the hospital," she said.

"What?" I said. "Oh, oh, I've got to get dressed, I'll take a shower, no, I'll get dressed. What? What? Should I take a shower or should I just get dressed? What should I do?"

"Just get dressed," she said.

"Okay, I'll get dressed. Do I wear a tie?" She was calm and cool and I was acting like a fruitcake.

I took her to the hospital, but back then, the whole idea of fathers even being around during a birth was that they were kind of a nuisance, let alone them being in the delivery room. Instead, you were with them off and on during labor, and then left behind when they went into the delivery room. The father's job was to pace around the waiting room with cigars in his pocket. As Frannie's labor dragged on, I told her, "I'm going to work for a while." I went home, took a shower, and went to work. At noon I returned to the hospital, but she still hadn't delivered the baby.

I was sitting next to her holding her hand and every time there was a contraction, she screamed and squeezed my hand. When I could get my hand back, I'd run down the hall for the doctor. By two o'clock in the afternoon, they were disgusted with me for running down the hall every ten minutes. Finally, at five o'clock, the doctor told Frannie she had to have a cesarean section.

We would have to wait a while, so I left the hospital and went to the Gaslight Club to meet my fraternity brother, Pete Castonguay, who was working for me at the time. He was the same guy who delivered the cleaning supplies for me back in college. I called Frannie's mother, Poopsie Belle, and let her know what was going on. Then I went back to the hospital to wait some more. The C-section was performed without complication and Jason was born. I was tickled to death to be a father.

We had decided to continue living downtown. Having a child wasn't going to change our lives, absolutely not. Not changing our lives, no, no, no. I'm telling you we had that bullshit discussion for months. What happened? We brought him home, laid him down in the middle of the living room, and counted his fingers. Yup, ten. Counted his toes. Yup, ten. Then we counted the toes again. He moved! How strong he was to move his head! This went on for months. Oh, Frannie, look at that eye contact, look at that. We'd have inane conversations for hours. No, the baby wasn't changing our lives at all.

So, we moved out of downtown Chicago.

The farther you go from city center the less expensive it is. We decided to look in Lake Forest, and that's where we found our house.

It was 8,000 square feet on four acres with a guesthouse, a greenhouse, and a pool, and it cost $160,000. Back then all you could finance on your mortgage was $100,000, so I put down $60,000 and we bought the house.

We were crazy about Jason, and Frannie was a wonderful mother. Wonderful. Any time you have kids, those are the best days of your life. Christmases and holidays are the best. In our neighborhood, everybody had a little bridge from the street to their house. At Halloween, the neighbors would put ghosts on pulleys across the street and play recordings of ghost sounds, and when the kids walked across the bridge, a hand would come up and touch them. It scared them silly, and I think we had more fun than the kids did. Everything we did was for the kids. We went to the Episcopal Church down the street, which was about a three-minute walk, and Jason was an acolyte. We had a home, a new baby, a good social life, and the business was doing fine.

Around this time, I also discovered Bruce Southworth, whom I met while he was doing the window displays at Sears in Chicago. His work was so good that I asked him if he'd like to organize a couple of parties for us. He was amazing and his parties were unbelievable. One year in the early '70s we had a big Fourth of July party where we had live tigers and elephants. There were hundreds of guests and everyone came dressed in red, white, and blue. We hired Elaine May to come and poke fun at everyone, and we had a great time.

Meanwhile that same night, those of us who were long on soybeans were celebrating because the price was going up and up. We were drinking cognac, talkin' big, and counting our money.

The next morning I woke up to the news that Nixon had embargoed the sale of soybeans to Japan. The US was a huge supplier of soybeans to Japan, so this meant the US was going to have a lot more soybeans on the market than it bargained for and soybean prices would go down. The US had a small crop that year, so my long position was profitable until then. But that Monday, soybeans went limit down—meaning they went down as much as they could in that trading session—and kept going that way for five days. I lost millions. Farmers lost millions, too; and they also lost in the long run because Japan went into the soybean business in Brazil in a big way. This was Nixon's way of controlling inflation and bringing domestic food prices down, which it did, but the repercussions are still being felt today. I read somewhere that protectionism is the gift that keeps on taking, and that's right.

18

THE GREAT GRAIN ROBBERY

In December of 1972, a brutal Siberian winter destroyed the Russian wheat crop. The next summer, Secretary of State Kissinger gave us the news that the US and the Soviet Union had signed the largest trade agreement ever made between the two nations. Previous agreements had kept grain sales to the Soviets confined to grain stored in US government elevators. The new deal now let them into our domestic markets, allowing the purchase of $750 million of grain over three years.

The Soviets started buying. By August they were having secret meetings with big American grain exporters and buying huge amounts of grain for future delivery. In September, the US government found out that the Soviets had already bought their full three years' worth. In fact, they had bought $770 million that crop year, which was way more than what the US was planning to export that year, plus 25 percent of the total US wheat crop and huge quantities of both soybeans and corn. Commodities skyrocketed and grain prices hit 125-year highs. By the next year, food prices themselves rose 50 percent. This became known as "The Great Grain Robbery." Refco made a fortune, which meant I made a fortune.

It was during this time that I first heard of Willard Sparks. He was from Dibble, Oklahoma, and had a PhD in agricultural economics from the University of Michigan. When he was a kid, another kid shot him in the eye with a BB gun. It was an accident, but he lost that eye. He was an upstanding Baptist who didn't smoke, drink, or cuss, but he had a weakness for the ladies. After a stint at the US Department of Agriculture, Sparks went to work for Cook Grain in Memphis for $25,000 a year as an ag-econ research guy. His job was to predict the size of crops and to estimate prices. The guy who was running Cook at the time left and went to work for Dreyfus Grain, leaving Cook without a president. Dreyfus Grain, by the way, is owned by the family of Julia Louis-Dreyfus who played Elaine on *Seinfeld*. Her great-great-grandfather, Léopold Louis-Dreyfus, started the Louis Dreyfus Company, a big commodities and shipping concern in France. Ned Cook, chairman of the company, asked Sparks to become the company's president.

"Nah," Sparks said. "I like doing research."

"I'll pay you $75,000 a year," Ned Cook told him. That was triple his salary!

"Nah," Sparks, said.

"Okay, $100,000," Ned said.

"Well," Sparks said. "I don't want to do it, but okay."

And with that Sparks became director of Cook's worldwide Agriproducts Group. Just a few months later, he got a call from the Russians. They thought Continental Grain and Cargill were gouging them, so they wanted to try Cook. They met at the Carlyle Hotel in New York City. Sparks had never been anywhere that fancy before. Hell, he thought his $25,000 salary was tall cotton.

Sparks asked the Russians how much grain they wanted and they told him. I don't recall the amount, but whatever it was, it was within their normal export allotment. Then they asked Sparks to come back the next day with a price.

The next morning on the way to breakfast, Sparks decided that he'd sell to them for 20 cents over the market. For example, if wheat was selling for $4.20 a bushel, he'd charge them $4.40. He sat down with the Russians and told them the price. Then they said they'd take *way* more than they originally stated. "What happened to what you said you wanted yesterday?" Sparks asked incredulously.

"Can you fill the order or can't you?" the Russian said.

Sparks knew that he was about to sell more grain than the entire US had available to export, and he was about to burst. He knew the deal would cause a grain shortage, which meant that grain prices would skyrocket.

"Okay," Sparks said, "but you can't buy anything from anybody else for two weeks, and you can't talk to anybody else for two weeks."

"Deal," the Russians said.

Sparks immediately had Cook start buying all the grain it could get its hands on. Not only did he plan to fill the Russians' order, but he knew that with American grain supplies depleted as a result, Cook would be able to sell their excess domestically for a hefty profit.

Then Cook started buying up all the barge freight, all the ocean freight, all the elevation, and all the trucking. The Russians had bought all this grain, and now Cook had to figure out a way to get it there while everybody else in the world got their goods delivered, too. Meanwhile, the US crops had a great year, and everybody in the market is a bear.

I started sniffing around. I talked to my friends on the wheat desk and they told me that wheat is okay, that it looked like it might go up.

I bought 500 or 600 contracts, and just my luck, it went straight down. So I asked 'em again, "What about the wheat?" and they said, "Don't worry." Next day, straight down again. Oh man. So I bought some more and asked again, "Is this ever going to be right?" Again he told me not to worry. Now I was really choking on it and out close to $2 million. The next day, boom, up, up, up. It kept going from $2.50 to $6 in a straight line. Soybeans went up from $2 to $12 in a straight line. It went crazy. It went up like that for about thirty days in a row, which for me meant about $600,000 a day. That was a good thing. In today's dollars, that'd be the equivalent of about $100 million.

Sparks couldn't believe how much money Cook made on that deal, and it put Cook on the map. That was "The Great Grain Robbery" and my introduction to the legendary Willard Sparks. He was famous in the commodities world and understood global agricultural systems better than anyone else. He was *the* authority on agricultural commodity analysis and research, and could walk into any cornfield and tell you what the yield was going to be. Until he died in 2001, he could stand up in front of a crowd and talk for three hours off the top of his head about the size and price of every crop in every country of the world.

When Cook went broke in about '78, I went down and hired fifty of their people, including Willard Sparks. Cook was a huge grain trader and I was a meat trader. Getting Willard and the Cook folks was a real boon for us and added a whole new dimension to Refco's capabilities.

19

LIFE WITH DAD
by Jason Dittmer

My earliest memories of my dad are from holidays, and my dad spanking me when I was bad, but what I remember most is my dad putting me to bed. I really remember that. His nickname for me was Studhorse. He wasn't much for reading stories, but he would talk about me and say how proud he was of me and how much he loved me. He was out of town a lot, but when he was home, he made it count. There was never any doubt in my mind that I was important to him. That was our time, in my room at bedtime, when no one else was around.

When I was about six years old, I played soccer. My dad had never played soccer in his life, but my mom had volunteered him to be a referee for one of my games. He walked out onto the field dressed in a full referee getup. He had everything from the black-and-white striped shirt to the pulled up black socks. So he looked the part, but he didn't understand the rules of soccer, so he blew the whistle once to start the game and basically it was just a shit show after that. Every time he'd make a bad call, the kids on my team would kick dirt on him.

I also played hockey, and he hated going to the games. One day we had a game in Champaign–Urbana, Illinois, and my dad said, "We're not driving." He put the entire team on his plane and flew us there. We hadn't won a game the entire season, so he thought it would be a quick trip, down and back in a day. We wound up being there for three days and winning the tournament. I remember him being proud, but also I remember him being a little irritated that a trip that was supposed to be six hours ended up being four days. Still, it was a big deal. All the kids thought flying in a private plane was just the best thing ever. He was always generous and supportive.

He was never short on affection and I never doubted his love for me. My dad didn't grow up with a dad of his own, so when I look back, I wonder how he learned how to be a good dad. You see so many people repeat the mistakes of their parents, so where did he learn how to be a dad? And he was a really, really good dad. I think now he probably wishes that he had been around more, but the truth is, as a kid you remember that you were together when it counted.

There is no doubt that when my dad met my mom, he fell in love with her. I think my mom fell in love with his ambition and his sense of humor. He was very charming. They clicked because of their senses of humor and their wanting the same things in life.

We grew up in a house with a lot of laughter and a lot of love. My dad did have his shortcomings in their relationship. I remember a story my mother told me when I was an adult, after they had been divorced for years. She said Dad told her that his list of priorities was business first, kids second, Mom third. I'm guessing he had been drinking at the time. Whether or not he said that I have no idea, but that was my mom's perception. I'm not sure that my dad, if he said it, meant to say it in that way. He likes to distill things down to black or white; he's uncomfortable with gray. He has to make lists and boil a situation down so that he can make sense of it. I think my mom felt like they should have been able to be successful in business and still live a balanced home life where he was around more.

20

ON MY OWN

We opened our New York office in 1973. I wanted to grow Refco and keep the money in the business, and Pop wanted to take it out and spend it, which was understandable because he was much older than I was.

"Pop," I said, "I want to buy you out."

"How do you want to do it?" he asked.

"I'll do a buy-sell. I'll say a price where I'll buy and if you want to sell it to me, sell it to me. Or, if you want to buy it, I'll sell it to you."

My price was $17 million, and he sold me his stake in the company in 1974. I owned 100 percent of Refco and Pop kept doing what he'd been doing for years, being a big broker. As part of the deal he also got to use the company planes for free, and I gave my mother and him free run of my house on Tarpon Island in Palm Beach, which was a four-acre private island.

When I bought Pop out, I had a big, hollow feeling in my stomach, a feeling of being utterly alone. He had taught me everything. He was the money behind everything. Without him, I wouldn't be anywhere.

★★★

In '75, Frannie and I bought our first house in Aspen, Colorado, with Chicago friends, Memrie and Perry Lewis. Those were happy times. Memrie was from Greenville, North Carolina, and later, encouraged by the designer David Easton, became a successful landscape designer.

There were a lot of Chicago people in Aspen so we had a bunch of friends there and made more as the years went on. It was also in '75 that I got my first jet, a Falcon 10. Before that I had owned a Duke and a King Air. With the jet, Chicago to Aspen was only a two-hour flight. Jason, and later our daughter, Alexis, went to summer camp in Aspen and loved it. Around '88 we sold that house to Memrie and Perry and bought another. The jet ended up going to Aspen at least fifty times a year. I wasn't always with them, but Frannie didn't care for commercial flights. The jet came in handy, especially after Frannie started collecting art and wanted to take her friends to art fairs around the country.

Also in '75, I started buying feedlots in Amarillo, Texas, with Paul Engler. Paul is a legend in the cattle business and probably the world's most famous cattle feeder. He started buying cattle when he was twelve years old. He enrolled in the University of Nebraska when he was just fifteen and paid for his education by selling cattle.

When we started Cactus Feeders, we had 100,000 acres in Texas at the Benjamin Ranch, and 75,000 acres in the Sand Hills of Nebraska. When we got up to 335,000 head in '85, we became the largest cattle-feeding operation in the world. Cactus Feeders today is still the biggest privately owned cattle-feeding company in the country, and one out of every twenty steaks eaten in America comes from there.

We used 40 million bushels of corn a year. We had 20,000 cattle a week come in, and 20,000 go out. To fatten them up, we had to feed them twice a day, within five minutes of the same time. A semi load of fat cattle is 40 head, and 40 into 20,000 means 500 trucks a week. The feeder cattle are 80 head a truck because they're little, so that's 750 trucks a week in and out. We'd generally have over 400,000 head at a time. Each one of them ate seven pounds of grain a day. That's a lot of feed.

We built our own railroad spur into the feed yard so we could bring a hundred-car train of corn a week out of Iowa. That's a long train. With our own spur we could unload the corn by releasing it from the bottom of the car, where it would go on an underground auger to the feed yard. No people, no trucks—efficient. Where the trucks did come in was to move the cattle when we bought and sold them. There were over a thousand trucks coming in and out of there every week. The logistics were difficult, but Paul was really good at managing it. We also traded a lot of cattle futures, because if you're in the cattle business, you've got to hedge them. You've got to buy corn, and you've got to buy feeder cattle. It's a huge operation.

Around that same time, we started Refco Capital Corporation to run our finance and treasury functions. We had figured out that the bank, in this case Chase Manhattan, was making more money on our cattle-feeding operation than we were. If they were charging us 8 percent on the $1,000 we borrowed from them to buy an animal, it would come to $80 per head in interest for them, and we'd make $8. That disparity made it clear to me that we needed to be in the banking business.

I hired the banker Phil Bennett away from Chase Bank in 1981. Phil was from Gloucestershire, England, and had played rugby for Cambridge. In 1983, he became our CFO at Refco. We started financing our own cattle and made tons of money. So we had the feedlot, the bank to finance them, and all the futures to hedge them. It was a sweet deal and a dynamic trade to say the least.

★★★

I had just bought my Falcon 10 jet, and the Lewises and Frannie and I decided to go to Bozeman, Montana, to learn how to rope cattle. I'd never roped before. I'd ridden plenty of horses but never roped. I had the outfit, though. I was wearing my gold Rolex, my Resistol hat, my bolo tie, my Red River vest, Lucchese boots, and a big belt buckle. I was the cowboy, man.

We flew from Chicago to Bozeman, and we'd been doing some drinking on the way. We landed in Bozeman and looked around for Jamie, Perry Lewis's cousin, but he wasn't there. I walked into the terminal, and it was all but empty because there weren't a lot of private planes going into Bozeman in 1975. The only person in there was this little Japanese guy with nineteen cameras around his neck.

"Hey, mister," he said as he tugged on my sleeve.

"You talking to me?" I asked in my best John Wayne voice.

"Yeah, you. You the driver of the Yellowstone bus?"

There went my ego.

Unfortunately, Jamie came around the corner and heard what the Japanese fellow had said to me. He didn't say a word then, but that night, Jamie had all his friends and neighbors over for a big barbecue, and that's when he decided to tell the story of "You the driver of the Yellowstone bus?"

The next day it went from bad to worse. We had our initial roping lesson. Then they opened the chute and out came the calves. We were going to learn how to head and heel them. This went on for four days, five hours a day, and in all that time I lassoed zero cows. Zero. I mean the rope hit them, but that was it. On the last day, Jamie took me to the dairy barn, where all the cows were in a pen—not running, just standing there.

"Rope a cow," he said. I threw the rope, and boom! Rope hits the ground. Boom! Ground again. I didn't catch any of those, either. But at least I had the outfit.

★★★

Frannie got pregnant again soon after that, and in December 1976, our daughter Alexis was born. She was gorgeous! We had three-year-old Jason and newborn Alexis and it just doesn't get any better than that. This was my family and this was what life was all about.

It was important to us that we had dinner together around the dining room table. I remember once when Jason was about five years old and we were having dinner and talking, Jason said, "You know, Mom doesn't really do anything. She just hangs around the house all day and plays tennis."

"Oh, really," said Frannie. "And what does Daddy do?"

Jason thought about this for a moment, then said, "Well, every day he gets up real early and drives to his office and sits behind a big desk . . . and hopes for the best."

Frannie and I couldn't stop laughing because it was true! Let me tell you something, the happiest time in your life is when you have little kids.

21

MY PARENTS
by Alexis Dittmer

My parents came of age in a time where there were opportunities everywhere and anything seemed possible. I don't think we can say that now. I don't think it's that easy anymore.

Both of my parents are such interesting, vibrant people. Both are profoundly creative. I'd go over to my friends' houses and think, *Wow, this is pretty lackluster.* Or there would be a crazy mom or abusive father. There was no vitriol in our family, and we were so lucky to grow up with two parents who really loved each other. You could feel it and see it. It shaped me in a great way. They both traveled a lot, especially my father, so he wasn't the kind of dad who was always taking me to soccer practice, but he was always very affectionate. He was different at home from how he was at the office, where he swore and ranted and raved. When he came home he shed his office persona. He had a tremendous ability to make me feel loved. Just as my father has great instincts about business, he also has great instincts about parenting.

I remember being about five or six years old and entering a swimming race. Just before the race, I decided I didn't want to do it. I think I was afraid of not winning. My dad and mother both said I had to do it. I got in the pool and I won.

I played tennis growing up, and every summer my father and I entered a father-daughter tournament at the country club. He didn't particularly want to play, but he still did it. In one tournament we were playing against the minister of our church and his daughter. The priest was cheating so badly that we had to call a line judge. My mother and Aunt Marilyn were watching the match, and finally they came down and got into it. I was a pretty good player, and I guess the priest couldn't stand being beaten by a child. I couldn't believe that this person who was a member of our community and the leader of our church was cheating. It was so egregious that my father just laughed.

My parents had such affection for each other. It was a nice thing to experience. I never realized until I was an adult how rare that is. They loved each other so much. Their energy together was amazing. They laughed a lot together, and when it was good, it was amazing to see. When they didn't agree, neither of them would back down. Once we were driving home from the movies and we were on the expressway in Chicago and my parents got into it. My mother made my father stop the car, and she walked the last few miles home. But most of the time they had fun together. I honestly think they had more fun than anybody.

We always had to be home for dinner, and we'd all sit down together and actually talk. My parents were never afraid to show their love for us. My father—and you'll hear this from a lot of people—has such a generosity of spirit. I was so lucky, and I really didn't appreciate it until I was an adult. My mother never criticized my body; my father never said damaging things to me. They just never, ever said anything that might make me feel not great about myself.

People ask me—and this comes up a lot—how did you end up so normal, because you didn't have a typical childhood? I'm normal, I'm nice, and I'm not fucked up or on drugs. People have said, "You grew up with chauffeurs and butlers and private jets. You should be an entitled asshole, but you're not." I'm that way because I had good parents. We had an extravagant lifestyle, but we weren't really affected by it because my parents were normal, nice people. My father impressed upon us that having all the stuff didn't make us special.

22

REFCO TAKES OFF

The year 1979 put Refco on the map. We'd been long on cattle starting around 1977. All the research was saying that we were going to have the smallest cattle supply in the last thirty years, and that cattle that was at $40 should go to $80. By 1979 we were long so much that the Exchange called me daily to ask what percentage of the open interest Refco had. "You tell me," I'd say.

"You have 80 percent of the open interest on April cattle," they'd tell me. "You have 40 percent of the open interest in the entire cattle trade."

"Okay, so . . . ?"

"You're just too big."

"Yeah," I'd say. "But we're right."

Years later, on one of my first dates with my current wife, Frances Schultz, a.k.a. "F-2," she asked me if I really did try to corner the cattle market. Obviously she'd been checking up on me.

"No!" I told her. "I *did* corner the cattle market."

In 1979, our clients netted $500 million after commissions. The brokers also made millions, and Refco netted $30 million itself. I don't think that's happened any place in the commodities business before or since. We made a fortune for our customers and everybody heard about it, and that was really exciting.

I've always believed that there are no higher callings in life than creating jobs for people and raising kids. I want everybody to do well. By the '80s, our business was exploding. We expanded and opened offices in Singapore, Hong Kong, New York, Rome, Jakarta, Amsterdam, Barcelona, Hamburg, Paris, and London. I had 1,000 brokers on commission and about 1,000 other employees, which was a very efficient ratio. Everybody was making good money. We had over 150 membership seats on exchanges around the world. I would buy the seats at $400,000 each and those guys could make $1,000,000 or more a year. To this day, there are fifteen or twenty guys who get together for drinks twice a year and get me on the phone. They tell me that if it hadn't been for Refco, none of them would have had the families they had and college-educated kids, and that their time with Refco was the most fun they'd ever had.

The 1979 Chicago blizzard was the second largest snowstorm ever to hit Chicago. Twenty-one inches of snow fell in just two days. O'Hare was closed for days, the train tracks were frozen, and the snowplows couldn't keep up. Right after that was when Frannie and I bought Tarpon Island in Florida. I never did like it there—I'm not a sea-and-sand type of guy—but the kids loved it and so did my parents. I eventually gave it to Pop.

I had two Rolls Royces: a convertible and a Silver Cloud limo, both given to me by my ski instructor, Mike Annan, because he made so much money trading with me. I used to drive the convertible over the bridge from Palm Beach to Tarpon Island, and I once saw a young boy fishing off the bridge. I learned thirty-some years later that kid was Billy Hurbaugh. I would meet him in Santa Ynez when he moved there with his husband, Randall Day, the rector of our local St. Mark's Episcopal Church. It turns out that they would both become very important to me. Funny how that works.

Randy Kreiling was from Peoria, Illinois, and one of the handsomest guys ever, just a stud. He was married to Helen, who was Bunker and Herbert Hunt's niece. Randy was hustling business for the Hunt brothers, and I was hustling him. When he moved from Dallas to Chicago, I gave him office space. That's when the Hunts decided they were going to squeeze the silver market, meaning they were going to buy up all the silver they could and make the price go up.

Bunker and Herbert Hunt were the sons of H. L. Hunt. H. L. started out as a dishwasher, learned to play poker, won his first oil lease in a poker game, and went on to become one of the richest men in America.

The Hunt brothers started buying silver in the early '70s when silver was $1.50 an ounce. Early in 1974, after they had amassed about forty million ounces of silver—8 percent of the global supply—they decided to ship it all to Switzerland. Before the silver was shipped, Randy Kreiling and his brother, Tilmon, held a shooting contest with a group of cowboys on the Circle K Ranch. They picked the twelve best marksmen. Randy, Tilmon, and the cowboys flew in the middle of the night on three chartered 707 jets to Chicago and New York. They loaded up the planes with the Hunts' silver—one of the largest silver transfers ever—and flew to Switzerland.

Now, Refco then was a relatively small business with maybe $10 million in capital. At the time, the capital requirement for a trade was around 6 percent. So if all our customers combined were trading, say,

$100 million in commodities, Refco would have to have $6 million in capital. The Hunts were putting up maybe $200 million on margin to trade the silver, and that was in addition to all of our other customers' trades. Hell, we had to go out and raise money just to have enough capital on hand. By January 1980, silver was at $50 an ounce. On January 21, the Board of Trade suspended silver trading. On March 27, which was called "Silver Thursday," silver opened at $15.80 and closed at $10.80, and the Hunts lost a lot of money. Since they traded some of that through Refco, Refco didn't participate in the trade. Refco never traded for itself. I traded for myself but not in this silver trade. And this, by the way, was when I stopped trading from the floor and started calling in trades from my office. Anybody could walk by and hear me on the floor, and obviously I didn't want that.

23

THE RUSSIAN GRAIN EMBARGO

On January 4, 1980, Frannie and I were hosting a big, fancy dinner party at the house in Lake Forest. I was short to the gills on corn and wheat and losing big at the time, like $4 or $5 million. I get a call from Rick Kaplan who was then the executive producer for ABC News. Rick was from Chicago and I met him through a friend in Washington and we became good friends. He went on to become president of CNN under Ted Turner, then later president of MSNBC. The Soviets had invaded Afghanistan, and Rick told me that they were preparing for the broadcast of President Carter's response that night. He thought Carter was going to impose a grain embargo against the Russians, and the guys in the newsroom were preparing charts to show how an embargo might affect the American farmer.

"What are you talking about?" I say. "He can't embargo the fucking grain. There's no one to sell it to except the Russians." By rights of course he told me this after the market had closed, but it didn't matter because my position was already in place.

"Well," Rick said, "that's what he's going to say."

I called up Willard Sparks, who was short up to his ass, too.

"Is there any chance that there's a grain embargo?" I asked him.

"Who you gonna sell it to?" he said.

"Right," I said. "Let's get Victor Pershing on the phone." Victor was the head of the Export Club of Russia and ran all the Russian grain imports. I figured the White House had Victor's phone bugged, but the three of us got on the phone anyway.

"Victor, any chance of a Russian grain embargo?" I asked.

"Who you gonna sell it to?" he answered. We hung up.

I was trying my best to be a good host at our dinner party, but I was choking on my trade and running in and out of the dining room, back and forth between the phone and the television, to see if President Carter was actually going to announce a grain embargo. No one could believe it because it was an economically stupid move.

Nevertheless, the embargo happened and they closed the exchange for five days. Obviously prices plummeted when they reopened the market. I made $53 million the first day. Jimmy Carter was my favorite president because he did everything wrong, and I made a lot of money. Reagan, however, almost killed me.

Rick was returning the favor of a little news scoop I'd given him some months earlier about the Russians in Iran. In 1979, Iran's Shia Republic came to power and aggravated relations with Sunni-ruled Iraq. I called Rick. "Tell me about the Russian tanks in Iran," I said.

"There aren't any Russian tanks in Iran," he told me.

But there were and here's how I knew: my guy at Fiat in Italy. Italian car manufacturers had great information because the Italians had great intelligence. Do you know the name of the Italian intelligence agency? Me either. Nobody does. American car manufacturers weren't doing business in Russia, but the Italians were. I had spoken to my contact at Fiat who told me about the Soviet tanks in Iran and that it was just kind of a fuck-you move. The Russians wanted to send a message.

Rick got off the phone with me and went to his bosses and said, "What about the Russian tanks in Iran?"

"There aren't any Russian tanks in Iran, get outta here."

A day later they came back to Rick and said, "Where'd you get that information?"

"I have sources," he said.

"Well, they were good sources because the Russians are in Iran."

24

CUBA, CASTRO,
AND A NEW HOUSE

Another lucrative deal in the 1980s was trading with Russia. US companies were forbidden to trade directly with the Soviets, but Refco London was a separate entity. We financed the Soviets' oil-for-sugar swap with Cuba.

Cuba gave Russia sugar and Russia gave Cuba oil. No one would take Cuban credit, so the Russians had to finance the Cubans. If you were to loan the Russians money, they might pay you 10 percent interest on January 1. The fact that interest rates were 2 percent wouldn't matter to them. It wasn't in their mentality. They didn't know what interest was. There's no word for risk in the Russian language. That became a huge trade for us.

The year 1980 marked the twentieth anniversary of the Cuban Sugar Company, which had been nationalized under Fidel Castro. I had just gotten my Falcon 50, and Frannie and I flew down to Havana. Travel between Cuba and the US was of course not allowed, but we could go as guests of the Cuban government provided we had the permission of the US government, which we did. We stayed at the Hotel Nacional de Cuba, a beautiful hotel in its day. It opened in the '30s and was a getaway spot both for celebrities and organized crime types. When we got there it was a shithole and still had bullet holes in it dating back to the 1933 rebellion. The first night of the anniversary party was a big deal simply because Cuban sugar was a big deal, and there were hundreds of people in the room. A guy walked up to me and asked if I was the person who owned the Falcon 50. I told him yes, and he said President Castro wanted to meet me. "Will you come with me?" he said.

Hell, I didn't know what they wanted, or if I was being set up or what. "Frannie, honey, if I'm not back in two hours, get the pilots and get the fuck out of here." I was dead serious.

I followed this guy to a private room where there were about thirty people, and Castro walked over.

"You came down in the Falcon 50?" he asked.

"Yes, sir."

"It's wonderful," he said. "Can I take a look at it?"

"Sure, Mr. President, you sure can. You just contact my pilots and the airport and we'll do it."

I went back to Frannie in the dining room and we we're seated next to the kitchen where every time the door opened it went *bang!* against my chair. *Bang!* All night long. The next night we were moved to a table in the center of the room, right in front of the head table. The night after that, we were at the head table, for no reason other than Castro wanted to see my plane. Frannie and I had a good laugh about that. I saw him three or four times after that, and we gave a dinner for him at our house in New York when he was in town for a big UN event. Not because I was fond of him or even approved of him—I wasn't and I didn't—but Cuba gave Refco a ton of business.

While we were in Cuba we had an interpreter whose father had been a doctor and had left Cuba when Fulgencio Batista was in power. The interpreter had been going to Juilliard in New York when her father moved them back to Castro's Cuba. At the time we met her, she had a fifteen-year-old daughter who wanted to become a prostitute because she could make more money doing that than the $350 her mother made per year as an interpreter. I asked this woman why her father came back, and she told me that he believed in communism. When I left, I gave her $500 and she wept. She probably could have gone to jail for having US dollars, but she sure was grateful.

In 1981, Frannie wanted to redo the house, but I didn't want to put more money into it. So we looked around Lake Forest and found another house we liked. It had been designed by David Adler in the '20s and sat on thirty-five acres. It had a 17,000-square-foot main house, a gatehouse, guesthouse, tennis court, and two separate garages. We had to have our own snowplow because the driveway was a quarter of a mile long and the city didn't plow it. It also had a greenhouse that you could drive a truck underneath and load up plants without exposing them to the elements.

We bought it for $2 million and hired architect and designer David Easton to complete an extensive renovation. A year later we moved in and lived there until we moved to New York in 1994. There's a nice chapter on our house in David Easton's book, *Timeless Elegance*.

One Christmas, I decided to go to a Lake Forest car dealership to buy cars that I would give to Pop, Bruce Southworth, and Frannie's sister, Marilyn Holland, in addition to one for me. The dealer was offering the top-end Mercedes-Benz for $15,000. I told the guy I wanted four of them and asked what kind of a deal he could give me. The guy wouldn't deal, not at all. So I left and went to Arlington Motors in a nearby suburb.

"How many of the new Mercedes do you have?" I asked him.

"I've got four," he told me.

"Would you like to sell all four?" I asked.

"I'm dying to sell all four," he said.

"What kind of a deal will you give me?"

I bought all four cars for $14,000 each. He didn't even ask for money up-front. He sent the cars to my house and sent me a bill. I was happy, he was happy, and the dealer in Lake Forest lost out on a $56,000 sale. What a schmuck.

25

LONDON AND *KOMMERSANT*

What really made our London office work was the business we got from Marc Rich. He was a big customer of ours, and he made billions trading in oil and metals. Belgium-born and Jewish, Marc's family moved to the United States to escape the Nazis. Marc was a big supporter of Israel and gave Israeli causes millions over the years. He also sold oil to the Israelis. The problem was that the oil came from Iran, and the US had an oil embargo against Iran because they were holding American hostages at the time. Marc also sold oil to South Africa while we had sanctions against them. In 1983 he was indicted on sixty-five criminal counts including tax evasion, racketeering, and trading with the enemy. If they had convicted him, he would have been sentenced to three hundred years in prison. Instead he fled to Switzerland, eventually pleaded guilty to thirty-five counts of tax evasion, paid $90 million in fines, and remained a fugitive. He never came back to the States and was on the FBI's Most Wanted List for years. He didn't even come back for his daughter's funeral when she died of leukemia in 1996.

About a week after Marc moved to Switzerland, I called and told him I wanted to come to Zug to see him. I went, and while we were drinking coffee and smoking cigars, and I told him we could do all of his business out of our London office. London was separate from Refco US, so the US government couldn't get at his money. I asked for his business and he said okay, starting tomorrow. He ended up paying us $500,000 to $1 million a month in commissions. That put our London office on the map.

Marc's wife, Denise, the famous music impresario, was a big Clinton supporter and had given more than $1 million to the Democratic National Committee. She also gave $100,000 to Hillary Clinton's senate campaign, and $450,000 to the Clinton Library. On Bill Clinton's last day in office, in January 2001, he pardoned Marc Rich.

I called Marc to congratulate him. Then I called Denise a few months later. Then the FBI came to see me. They wanted to know if the Clinton Library was tied to the pardon.

"You talked to both of them," they told me. "Was there a connection?"

I had no idea. How would I know?

The first time Frannie and I went to Russia was in the late '70s. We took a train from Finland to Moscow and when we got off the train, we realized that everything we'd heard about Russia was propaganda and bullshit. America had to make the Soviets seem scary to justify increasing the US defense budget. But we could see for ourselves there was nothing there. They had no wealth, none. They didn't even have phone directories, although that didn't matter because hardly anyone had a phone. There were food shortages, empty shops, horrible transportation. The only ones who had anything were the elites, the politburo. There were no maps or golf courses because the Russians figured when the invasion came—any invasion—the enemy wouldn't be able to find anything or cross open land with tanks. No one played golf anyway. If you asked someone in the USSR to show you where he lived, he couldn't do it, because there were no maps.

I first heard about *Kommersant* in the late '80s through Ed Weidenfeld. Ed was a lawyer in Washington, DC, who specialized in estate and asset protection law and who had served as an advisor to three presidents. He also helped bring Major League Baseball back to Cuba after a forty-year absence, when the Baltimore Orioles played the Cuban national team in two exhibition games in the spring of 1999. Ed was (and still is) married to Sheila Rabb, who was First Lady Betty Ford's private secretary and whose father had served in the Eisenhower administration and as US ambassador to Italy under Ronald Reagan. Ed knew this guy, Craig Copetas, who was a journalist. Copetas had started out in the London bureau of *Rolling Stone,* and then went on to *Esquire* and others. Now, he was in Russia helping to put together the first independent business newspaper since the revolution.

"I think we could have some fun with this. Let's go to Russia and see what's going on," Ed said to me.

"Okay," I said, "good, and I can go see Victor Pershing at the Export Club and kill two birds with one stone." In those days all the grain bought and sold by Russia was done so by the government, and the Export Club was the government organization that handled it. Victor was head of it.

We went to Moscow and I met Vladimir Yakovlev, whom everyone called Volodya. He wanted to start a newspaper. His dad, Yegor Yakovlev, was a respected journalist and had been editor-in-chief of the *Moscow News*, so Volodya wasn't just some schmuck with an idea. He told me he could get writers from the *Moscow News*, put the paper together, sell advertising, and that was it. He didn't mention the shakedown part, where they would tell people they wanted to do an article on them, which could expose them in a negative light. But! For a large sum of money they could write a good story, and that's how they wrote stories after perestroika—it was all bought and paid for.

But I didn't know that then. "Okay," I said, "let's do it." I would get free advertising and a share of the profits, and I'd distribute the paper, translated into English, in the US. I gave them money and also equipment and supplies—$200,000 worth of batteries, old reel-to-reel tape recorders, and old model computers. Everything was old but they loved it. They thought it was cutting edge. They had an armed guard at the door to watch over all that old stuff we sent them.

The paper was called *Kommersant* after one originally published in 1909 that was shut down by the Bolsheviks. The first edition came out in December 1989, and it was the first private, post-revolution, business information newspaper in the country. It came out weekly and was a success from the beginning.

I'd go to Russia to visit the Export Club and to check on *Kommersant* in my Falcon 50. When I arrived at Sheremetyevo International Airport outside Moscow, there would be a line of limousines waiting for me. Russian made ZiLs, pretty nice cars actually. They would take me to a little fancy area, check my passport, and then they would get the code off the radar in my plane because they were afraid I might sell my radar to someone. After all that, I'd go outside, get into the limo, and I'd have a police motorcade to the city. I'd be thinking, *What the hell is this?* I was either by myself or with one or two others, and we'd all ride in the same car. It was goofy to have so many cars. They just wanted to make it look like a big, important entourage.

We'd go to a hotel that the average Russian couldn't afford, which was supposed to be a good hotel. At the end of the hall there was an old lady sitting there who would hand you your key. When you got in the room, there'd be a bare light bulb hanging from a string. I'm sure it was bugged. It was pretty damn bleak, I've got to say.

We'd go out to dinner and I was never sure exactly what we were eating. The food was so terrible, it's no wonder they drank vodka all the time. Some guy would come every morning about ten o'clock, bringing vodka, and they drank it like we would coffee. They also had a guy guarding the fax machine with a .45 pistol so we couldn't send out anything they didn't know about.

Volodya was a total scamp and ended up burning just about everyone. I had put about $500,000 into the paper, and I had a contract with Volodya for exclusive information marketing. Next thing I heard was that Volodya had secretly sold the paper for about $3 million to Jean-Louis Servan-Schreiber in Paris, where *Kommersant* was a big hit. I hired a lawyer, Jean de Hauteclocque, and it turned out there were two different versions of the contract. On the copy Volodya gave Servan-Schreiber, my name had been whited out and Servan-Schreiber's name written in. It wasn't even clever. A contract didn't mean anything in Russia back then.

I never saw a penny of my half million back. That probably goes without saying. But *Kommersant* was fun, and it still exists. Doing business with the Russians then was like . . . well, Volodya once told me to imagine that Al Capone had taken over the United States in 1917, killed anybody who had class and intelligence, and the thugs took all the power. That's what Russia is today.

I had a lot of the Russians from *Kommersant* come to my house in Lake Forest. They all had terrible teeth, so I paid for six or seven of them to get their teeth fixed. In Russia, they would do root canals with a paper clip and leave it in the tooth. My dentist called me up after seeing a few of these kids and said, "Where are you getting these people? I've never seen anything like this—I've never seen a piece of paper clip in a tooth."

"That's Russia," I said.

I tried to get Volodya to get his teeth fixed, but he wouldn't do it.

We brought more Russians over, a couple of thousand, to attend courses we were giving at Refco. They could do the most complicated mathematical formulas in their heads, but they could not grasp the concept of risk. It just didn't exist in their culture. They would come to class once, and then we never saw them again. All they wanted to do was buy stuff at sporting goods stores, drink, and chase girls. Then they all went back home to Russia.

26

THE HEADY YEARS

The 1980s were explosive years for us. We were pushing and shoving and getting big. After the 1979 cattle trade, the Commodity Futures Trading Commission was constantly investigating me. We had offices in fourteen countries and over 150 memberships in seven countries' exchanges, more than Goldman Sachs and Merrill Lynch had combined. We were trading everything from cattle to cocoa to oil to gold to currencies. We had two full-time meteorologists and thirty-three PhDs in agricultural economics on staff. No one else did that, not even Merrill Lynch, and they were the big guys on the block back then. We also hired gumshoe types to check on people we were doing business with or thought we might do business with.

Also in the '80s was the economic downturn. Paul Volcker, chairman of the Federal Reserve under Presidents Carter and Reagan, raised interest rates to 18 percent, which put a lot of our competitors out of business.

If you used to be able to finance 100 bushels of corn at 8 percent interest, and now it's at 18 percent, how much do you want to keep in storage? None. What happens to the price? It goes down. How many cattle do you want to feed? Not that many. How much gold do you want to hold? None. You don't want to hold anything. Volcker basically put everybody out of business. And that's when you buy businesses at bargain prices—in the bad years. So we bought BJ Land, Iowa Grain, Stotler & Co., Continental Grain, and a few others.

The '80s were heady years for us because of our size and the money we were making. I didn't have to ask for business anymore. People were calling me and asking if they could clear with Refco, just so they could access our research. We had quarterly research meetings in Memphis where all our brokers would come down from all over the country on their own dime. That's where Willard Sparks and our thirty-three researchers were based. We bought the brokers dinner, gave them a three-hour talk on what was going on, and everyone would be back home in time to go to work the next day. A lot of the guys had their own planes because Refco made more millionaires in the commodities business than anybody had ever done before.

The Commodities Futures Trading Commission (or CFTC) didn't like these meetings. They claimed we affected the market too much. "What?!" I'd say. "So, in other words, we shouldn't trade on research?"

"Well, we didn't say that. But can you have one meeting a year instead of one a quarter?"

"No," I'd say. "People pay us commissions because we give them the research."

The CFTC was always mad at us. When you think about it, do companies like Abbott, Pfizer, or Siemens want regulations? Yes, because regulations ratchet up the cost of entry and keep new players out of the game. The commodities business is the same. Merrill Lynch, PaineWebber, Lehman Brothers—none of those guys wanted us there. In 1969 Refco was just a footnote. We were no one. When we started making big money in the early '80s, it pissed off our competitors, who whined to the CFTC. Our customers weren't whining, though, because they were making money.

Merrill Lynch, PaineWebber, Lehman, all of them, went into the cattle-feeding business. And they all lost a fortune. But it wasn't their money, it was their customers' money. When they went broke—and it didn't take them long—we bought them out. The big difference between them and us was that it was Paul Engler's and my money that financed our feedlots, not my customers'.

It was also around 1980 that I made a big cotton trade. Cargill was hedging their cotton, meaning they were selling it short, betting that the price would go down. I bought. When the price started going up, they either had to buy back the contracts at a loss or deliver me the cotton. That's how it works. I took delivery of the cotton and sold it all to China. Cargill didn't like that, claimed I was invading their territory, and called me and told me so. I told them to go fuck themselves. That wasn't very smart of me.

Cargill, a global behemoth and the largest privately held corporation in terms of revenue in America, went to the CFTC and told them we were in their playpen and that they wanted us out. I made $18 million on the trade and incurred $12 million in legal fees to fight Cargill, even though I was in the right. But that's the price of doing business. Everybody is mad at you because you're not supposed to be competing with the big boys and beating them. But we did.

27

PARIS TO RUSSIA

Fay and David Peck were the reason that Frannie and I bought a house in Aspen. They invited us out there all the time, and that's how we came to like it so much. David had movie-star looks and Fay was an artist. He was a big executive at Lamb, Little & Co., the Chicago insurance firm. The Pecks were very fond of this kid, Tom Scichili, who was a contemporary and good friend of their own children. I thought a lot of the Pecks, and if they loved Tom Scichili, I knew there must be something good there.

When I first met Tom in Aspen in 1979, I thought he looked like a ski bum. My first impressions of him were completely wrong. He was in college studying economics and politics, and he was trading penny stocks. I talked to him for a while and he had the kind of cocky personality that I thought would work well in business. He was smart, tenacious, and confident. I told him, "I'll give you some of my own money to trade, and we'll set up the account at Refco." Penny stocks are not set up to make money except for the broker–dealer. I knew that, and I expected him to lose. I figured that even if he lost all the money, he would have learned something. But he didn't lose. He made money, and that's about a hundred-to-one shot.

Tom decided to go to law school and then landed a job working at a big law firm, but he wasn't happy. In 1986 he told me he wanted to move to France. We had opened our Paris office on the Rue Royale, in 1981, on the same day François Mitterrand was elected President. France had a big economy back then, and in February 1986 the Matif Paris futures market had just opened, which was the equivalent of the Chicago financial futures market. I offered Tom a job at the Paris office, got him a job trading French bond futures on the floor, and told him to learn French.

Tom quit his job and moved to France. The president of Refco Paris at the time was Alain Delchet, who later died from cancer at a young age. He was a wonderful man and a gentleman's gentleman. Alain met with Tom and sent him off to learn French over the summer, which he did. I had someone from Refco come to teach our traders the sign language that we used in the pits in Chicago, and Tom learned that, too. No one else was using sign language in France then; we were the first. They had just started trading bond futures in Paris and they were still trading stocks using chalkboards and telephones. Everyone in there smoked. It was crazy. And again, Tom made money.

Serge Versono, who had taken over our Paris office after Alain died, asked Tom to drum up some business with the market makers. He was successful at that too, winning over the big French banks like Crédit Lyonnais and BNP, and Credit Suisse First Boston in London as well. Spreads between British gilts and French bonds became an attractive trade, and soon Tom was making more money than Serge.

One day Richard Reinhart, the head of our London office, was visiting Paris, and he and Serge had been drinking at Maxim's, which was right by our office. Serge realized he had locked his keys in the office, but he could see that his window was open and figured he would climb out a hallway window, walk along the ledge, and climb into his office. The building was in a cobblestone courtyard that was locked after hours, but the courtyard, and therefore the building, was accessible via Maxim's. Richard was watching from the courtyard as Serge, in his expensive leather shoes, slipped and fell three floors to his death. The people in the trading room saw it too. It was horrible, and emergency services couldn't get to him because the courtyard was locked. Ironically, Serge's wife was a medical doctor and a beautiful, wonderful woman too. The worst part was that if Serge had just banged on the trading room door, someone would have let him into the office. But he'd had a few drinks.

Matif started to die down and finally emptied out. Maybe it's just as well. The good news/bad news about doing business in Paris then was that if you paid a guy $100,000 a year in commissions, you also had to give the government $100,000 a year. From 1987 to 1990 our taxes in France were so high that we could have bought a Gulfstream IV for $18 million, flown everybody to the Isle of Man every day, had them work out of there, and flown them back. And it still would have been cheaper than paying the taxes we paid.

When Tom Scichili left Refco, he started looking into opportunities in Russia. The Berlin Wall had come down in 1989 and Eastern Europe was changing fast. We had Michael Dee, an English businessman with extensive international experience, set up a partnership called Lake Forest Partners, and I put up a couple million dollars.

After Boris Yeltsin became president in 1991, he began to allow privatization in business so that the Soviets could move toward a market economy. The plan was to transfer shares to the Russian people by giving them vouchers for stock in the newly privatized companies. We started trading through a small broker-dealer that Tom had helped create called IFK Dilen. We bought those vouchers like crazy, and we bought Russian government bonds paying 60 to 80 percent, although they were denominated in rubles, which was a big risk. But if they paid, in two years we could get 120 percent on our money.

In those days nobody believed what the Russian government said, so most people thought the vouchers were a joke and sold them for peanuts. People would bring their vouchers to a ratty marketplace in an old convention hall, where they were traded in a flea-market–like atmosphere. We would buy them for pennies on the dollar, convert them into shares, and then, we hoped, trade the shares. There was also a crazy arbitrage trade from huge spreads between the price of Russian shares in privatized companies, which only Russians could own, and the much higher price of those same bundled shares trading in New York. After a while, people caught on to the vouchers, the arbitrage, and the bonds with the astronomical interest rates, and more and more people started buying them. One of the earliest and best known of them was Bill Browder of Hermitage Capital, who wrote the book *Red Notice.*

Then interest rates started going down. Everyone was getting nervous about the Russian markets. You were getting 20 percent on the bonds at that point, but it was in rubles and you still had to convert them to dollars. So what was going happen if the ruble went down? The whole thing would fall apart and wipe out the value of the bond. Meanwhile in '97, the Thai baht collapsed, there was a whole financial crisis in Asia, and the markets everywhere were shocked as a result. So I called Scichili and told him to sell everything in Russia. Twenty percent wasn't going to go on forever. That eliminated our risk, and we had done well. We had one broker-dealer who defaulted, but 90 percent of our trades cleared, and as we feared, the ruble collapsed in '98.

Michael Dee thought we should get out of there, but we didn't want to because we still had $100,000 or so invested in a large privatized Soviet–era laundry business. Dee told us just to write it off, but Tom said no because it was making a profit. Then he tried to sell it back to the Russians. "We'll give you $150,000 for it," they told Tom.

"No," said Tom, "it's worth more than that in real estate alone. Plus we have all these pickup locations, and we're investing and converting it into a modern dry cleaning business. No. It's worth much more."

"You don't understand," they said. "Do you want the $150,000 or do we just take it?"

Tom tried haggling for about ten minutes, but then he took the money. That's what Russia was like back then. By the way, the sub-title of Bill Browder's book *Red Notice* is *A True Story of High Finance, Murder, and One Man's Fight for Justice.* Anyone who's ever doubted that dealing with Russians in business—some Russians anyway—is risky, if not downright dangerous, needs to read this book. It's terrifying.

We liquidated Lake Forest Partners, and Michael Dee was surprised that we came back with any money at all. Tom made money in a place where it wasn't supposed to happen, and the fact that we all made money and got out of there unscathed was amazing.

28

GEORGE BARLEY

George Barley was from Orlando, Florida. He was a Harvard graduate, real-estate developer, and an activist for the preservation of the Florida Everglades. One day in 1982 I got a call from George. We had a mutual friend in Tom Lewis, whom I'd met years ago when he was dating a daughter of my friend Stan Rumbough.

"Tom Lewis told me to call you to invite you to a pheasant shoot I'm hosting in England. Do you have a pair of guns?" he asked.

"I sure do, two Remington 1100 shotguns."

"No. You can't shoot those. Do you have an over-and-under or a side-by-side?"

"No."

"Well, you've got to get two because there's a loader, a guy who loads one of your guns while you shoot the other."

"Where do I get over-and-unders?"

"Go to Purdy's or Holland and Holland in London before you come to the shoot. Ah, hell. I'll meet you there. Do you have the right hunting clothes?"

"Yeah, I've got blue jeans and boots."

"No, no, no, no, no. Do you have plus fours? Or Wellingtons?"

"No, of course not."

"Never mind. I'll get you outfitted."

George and I were staying at Claridge's in London. We went shopping and I got the short pants, long boots, jacket, hat—the whole deal to go shooting—plus a $50,000 pair of shotguns, and they were the cheap ones. I have no idea why English shotguns cost so much, even if they are handmade and hand-engraved, but they do. The next day we drove up to the shoot in Newcastle, to Biddick Hall, the private lodge of the Earl of Durham, on the grounds of Lambton Estates. This marked the beginning of my adventures with George Barley, which only got worse from there.

George would plan these trips, helping himself to my plane and everything else. Then he would call me up and tell me where we were going and when we were leaving. I mean, he was shameless! I'd always say, "No, no, no, not doing it," and then I'd end up doing it anyway.

"I've got an idea," George told me once. "I have an invitation to go shoot doves with King Hassan of Morocco and Juan Carlos, the king of Spain. We'll stay at La Mamounia in Marrakech, and we'll have a ball."

"George, I'm not going!"

"I've already talked to your pilots, I've got the caviar coming and we're leaving at four o'clock, two weeks from today."

"I am not doing this!"

"It's already done."

I did it and I had the best time. After that we went to the cork country in Portugal. "George, no," I said. "All we do is shoot and it costs a fortune!" Of course we went, and that's when the Spanish Riding School gave its private performance for us at lunch—all sixteen of us, including King Constantine of Greece and his wife.

Another time George and I were on the Rovos Rail train, a luxury
train that runs 3,000 miles around South Africa. There was a bar car,
a dining car, sleeping cars, and it was all very fancy. We would get off
the train after breakfast, get on horses with our shotguns in scabbards
attached to the saddles, and gallop off to shoot birds. A line of boys and
men, called beaters, would walk across the field hooting and shouting
and flushing the birds so they'd fly up, and we'd shoot. We'd have
lunch in the field, get back on the train, the train would take off, and
we'd do it all again the next day.

On the train with us was Patrick Mavros, a silversmith and jew-
eler from Zimbabwe. He's an interesting guy—a fifth generation
Zimbabwean, and everyone else in his family is a doctor. As our trip
was ending I gave Patrick my card and told him that if he was ever in
the States, to give me a call.

"Refco," he said as he looked at my card. "Refco. Your dad's name
is Ray, your mother is Evelyn."

"How do you know that?"

"A few years ago I was down in Acapulco having drinks with them
around a big table with a bunch of people," Patrick said. "Ray asked
me where I was from and I said Zimbabwe. He turned to your mother
and said, 'Evelyn, do we have an office in Zimbabwe?' Then this went
on and on as Ray asked everyone at the table where they were from.
Then he'd ask your mother, 'Evelyn, do we have an office in . . . ?'"

I was laughing because it sounded just like Pop. "Listen," I told
Patrick. "I'm giving a party for Pop's seventieth birthday, and if you're
in the States, you have to come by." As it turned out, he did. It was
1983 and Bruce Southworth had cooked up a great trading-themed
party with quote boards and telephones at every table and directories
listing the phone numbers of the other tables. They were supposed to
be used for trading, but everyone used them to talk dirty to the other

guests, saying stuff like, "I've always wanted to sleep with you," because no one knew who was calling. People also got up to talk about Pop and it was great. Then I had Patrick get up. Pop didn't recognize him earlier in the night, so it was a big surprise. Patrick gave a little speech about how he and Pop met. Everyone laughed like crazy because that was exactly what Pop did.

Today Patrick has a shop on the Fulham Road in London and is still making beautiful pieces inspired by his native Africa. Kate, the Duchess of Cambridge, is a customer, so he's very popular. Patrick was one of the many bona fide characters I met in my adventures with George Barley.

Sadly, George died in 1995 in a plane crash on the way to talk to the Army Corps of Engineers about the restoration of the Everglades. George was one of the greatest guys I've ever met, and I miss him dearly.

My grandmother, Osa Newman Robertson, and her baby girl, my mother Evelyn Jewel, circa 1925. Grandmother Osa died in 1936. COURTESY SUSAN ROBERTSON.

This is what the Chicago wheat pit looked like around 1920. At the top left you can see where the prices were recorded on a chalkboard. The technology and the dress code changed over the years, but the chaos and cacophony of the open outcry trading pits remained for nearly a century more. EVERETT HISTORICAL/SHUTTERSTOCK.COM.

My mother and biological father, Marlin Dittmer. In this picture, I look to be about a year old, so this would also have been around the time my parents divorced. Marlin enlisted in the Navy not long after I was born and served in the Pacific during World War II. I only saw him a handful of times throughout my life.

With my Aunt Myrtle Dittmer. Aunt Myrtle never married and lived across the street from the Lutheran church in Le Mars, Iowa, until she died at 103. We Dittmers are of hearty stock.

My mother said I looked like one of the "Dead End Kids" in this picture, referencing a 1935 Sidney Kingsley play by the same name that was later made into the movie *Dead End*. The story was about a bunch of children growing up on the streets of New York.

Grandpa JJ Robertson gripping the day's quarry and my uncle, Paul Robertson, with the famously aromatic coon dog Ring, on the Haywarden, Iowa, family farm, which was technically just across the border in South Dakota.

In the sacred cowboy suit with my Great Uncle Henry Dittmer, whom we all called "Grandpa Dittmer." My father Marlin promised me a red cowboy suit, and neither he nor the cowboy suit ever came. I pestered my mother about it so much that she finally bought it herself, and told me it was from him.

A school photo from the fifth or sixth grade, inscribed by my mother, "This looks like Honor Guard material doesn't it?"

TOM DITTMER, *President*

From a University of Iowa Sigma Phi Epsilon fraternity yearbook. In addition to being in ROTC, I was president of my fraternity my senior year, and ran a little cleaning supplies business on the side. I did whatever I could to earn spending money.

Mother and Ray Friedman, whom I called Pop, were married in 1959. Here they are with me just after ROTC graduation from the University of Iowa in 1964. My mother cried for a week afterward, in utter shock and relief that I had actually graduated.

On *The Ed Sullivan Show* as officer-in-charge of the US Army Drill Team, a precision drill platoon of the 3d Infantry Regiment, also known as the Old Guard. Sometimes in practice, just to razz me, the guys would knock my hat off with the bayonets as they tossed them overhead. All the same, we'd cut coffee cans in half and put them inside our caps for protection, just in case. Fortunately the TV performance went off without a hitch.

The ceremonial duties of the 3d Infantry Honor Guard included guarding the Tomb of the Unknown Solider, overseeing burials at Arlington, and attending state funerals. Following the funeral of Ambassador Adlai Stevenson in 1965, I was officer-in-charge of overseeing his casket aboard the presidential plane to return to his home state of Illinois.
US ARMY PHOTOGRAPH.

LEFT: Standing on Jackson Street at the foot of LaSalle Street, the formidable Chicago Board of Trade building was the tallest in Chicago from 1930 until 1965. Atop the building is a three-story aluminum statue of Ceres, the goddess of grain. It was declared a National Historic Landmark in 1978 today is the primary trading venue for the CME Group, formed in 2007 by the merging of the CBOT and the Chicago Mercantile Exchange.
COURTESY OF JOE RAVI/SHUTTERSTOCK.COM.

BOTTOM: Trading floor of the Chicago Board of Trade, 1965. Foreground shows oats pit; behind and to the left, wheat pit; at right edge corn pit; and soybean pit beyond. People on the catwalk around the perimeter recorded prices on chalkboards.
COURTESY OF PHOTOQUEST/GETTY IMAGES.

Trading floor of the Chicago Board of Trade, 1973. Chalkboards were still in use but electronics were starting to replace them. In those days, traders would do crazy things, like walk into the exchange shaking out an umbrella they had run water over in the bathroom—and the market would break! No wonder commodities traders had the reputations they did. Courtesy of the US Department of Agriculture.

Tall, good-looking, funny, and smart, Frances Ronshausen was the girl of my dreams. We married in 1966 in her hometown of Port Arthur, Texas. Little did I know we would return there so soon after the disastrous (but hilarious in hindsight) curtailment of our honeymoon. Courtesy of Watkins Studio.

Guess who's coming to dinner?

We feel there's a Bear Market ahead in cattle . . . will you be prepared for the price break? Study our **FREE** complete 3-page cattle report and detailed market analysis information, to protect your cattle-feeding profits from our projected price decline. Direct from the floor, we can alert you to advice and analysis, while feeling the pulse of the cattle-feeding and packing industries. With professional personalized service, and associate offices in all major livestock terminals, we can help you "bear" it!

DITTMER TRADING COMPANY
SUITE 1303 · 110 NORTH FRANKLIN ST.
CHICAGO, ILLINOIS 60606 · (312) 236-0669

MEMBER: CHICAGO MERCANTILE EXCHANGE

From my pre–Refco days as a trader, a flier for the short-lived Dittmer Trading Company.

Our young family: Frannie, Jason, Alexis, and me. The happiest time of my life.

From the left: Pop, Abigail ("Dear Abby") Van Buren, née Friedman, and Mother. Pop, Abby, and her twin sister and competing advice columnist Ann Landers, were first cousins. Growing up, "Popo" (Abby) and "Eppie" (Ann) were known as the Friedman Twins from Sioux City.

A long way from Haywarden. The second, and last, house we lived in in Lake Forest was designed by architect David Adler and sat on thirty-five acres.

TOP: Taking a break from pheasant shooting at Biddick Hall in County Durham, England, sometime in the eighties. From left are my old Chicago friend Barry MacLean; George Barley who introduced me to English shooting; me; and longtime friend Tom Lewis.

CENTER: With my Sioux City High School pal film producer Jeff Pill, and the Falcon 50 I bought in 1980.

BOTTOM: Through our London office, Refco handled sugar trading for Cuba, and it was big business for us. When the Cuban government invited me to the twentieth anniversary of the Cuban state sugar company, Frannie and I went. President Castro was fascinated by my airplane and asked to see it. What could I say? I was not a fan of his, but I did appreciate the hospitality—and Cuba's trading business of course.

TOP: The craziness and the chaos of the open outcry trading pits, with a sign language, behavior, and dress code all its own, now all in the past. Every trader wore a certain color jacket signifying the company he worked for, and a badge with his own initials, which became the basis for a nickname. My initials, THD, turned into "Thunder," and that's what they called me. Well, they called me worse than that sometimes, too. COURTESY OF GETTY IMAGES.

BOTTOM: The chalk boards listing prices were long since replaced with flashing lights and digital read-outs at the Chicago Mercantile Exchange on South Wacker Drive, pictured here before its 2007 merger with the CBOT and subsequent moving of its operations to that building on Jackson and LaSalle streets. COURTESY OF JOSEPH SOHM/SHUTTERSTOCK.COM.

The New York Mercantile Exchange, with Refco's booth visible in the foreground. I wanted to move to New York in the eighties, but Frannie balked. Finally in '94 we did move, but she was never happy there.
COURTESY OF MATT PIRINEA.

TOP: Mom and Pop at a party in Palm Beach. They loved it there and were very social.

BOTTOM: Souvenir from another trip to Cuba, this time with TV news producer Rick Kaplan. Rick had bought a duffle bag full of Cuban cigars, which he then had nerve to ask Castro to sign for him. When the customs agent discovered the cigars and asked what they were, Rick responded, "Gifts." The customs guy couldn't believe it when he saw that each box was signed by Fidel Castro. "Who *are* you?" he asked.

TOP: For about the best anniversary celebration you could imagine, my friend Bruce Southworth organized a cruise for one hundred of our closest friends on the *Sea Goddess*, which included a dinner dance in the amphitheater at Ephesus, Turkey, and a private concert with Diana Ross in Venice. A few months later, after thirty years of marriage, Frannie and I separated.

LEFT: I gave up car racing for motorcycles and enjoyed touring in Europe with my biking buddies. I've since given that up, too. Your reflexes diminish with age, and motorcycles at high speeds leave no margin for error.

LEFT: *Rancho la Zaca*, the ranch and vineyard in the Santa Ynez Valley of California, near Santa Barbara, where I live today with my wife Frances Schultz. I'd always thought this area was the prettiest ranch country I'd ever seen, and it was my dream one day to live there. The house was designed by Hugh Newell Jacobsen for the actor James Garner and his wife. The property has a pond, a sporting clays range, and a rodeo ring, and it's been great having friends and family visit through the years.

COURTESY OF JEREMY BALL.

RIGHT: Frances and me before a party at the ranch. We do a lot of entertaining together there, and life is good.

COURTESY OF LAUREN PORCHER.

BOTTOM: Together ten years and counting, Frances Schultz and I were married at the ranch in 2012. Here we are with both our families, and we've since added a granddaughter.

COURTESY OF AARON DELESIE.

29

JERRY GOULD

Jerry Gould, a PhD and professor emeritus at the Graduate School of Business at the University of Chicago, was another guy who changed my life for the better. Jerry taught applied mathematics and management science and he used to tell me, "All math PhDs wanted to be physicists but couldn't make it." He was a really funny guy and he used to laugh when his students would give him bad reviews after his lectures. They would call him the most arrogant, dumb sonofabitch they'd ever seen, and Jerry would laugh like crazy. He built a system so he could trade the market and beat it. I put up the money. He traded, it didn't work, and he lost it all in just a few days. Then he built a system for stocks, which did work. I loaned him the money to start the business and I got half the business. I wound up making a million-some bucks from it when it was eventually bought by Fidelity.

Jerry introduced me to a group of guys at the University of Chicago, School of Economics, and these guys were all geniuses: Milton Friedman, Arthur Laffer, Gary Becker, and Merton Miller.

Milton Friedman, Nobel Prize winner in Economic Sciences, was probably the most influential economist in the world at the time. He was an advisor to President Reagan and British Prime Minister Margaret Thatcher, and he was a big advocate of the free market. Friedman, with the help of the Ford Foundation, made it possible for thirty young students, called the Chicago Boys, from Santiago's Universidad Católica in Chile, to come to America and study "monetarism" with Friedman and his group of economists. Monetarism is basically a macroeconomic view that inflation depends on how much money the government prints. Basic Econ 101.

The Chicago Boys returned to Chile after the Pinochet coup and put Friedman's free-market reforms system to work, which is why Chile has a good economic system today. Their Social Security is privatized. You buy stocks with your money. You don't give it to the government for them to spend and issue you an IOU; your money actually exists. You want to borrow from your Social Security to buy a house? Fine. The money is actually there. Imagine, the average Chilean now retires with 80 percent of what the average American retires with, and their system didn't begin until 1980. Those guys went back home and changed Chile forever.

Arthur Laffer was a two-term member of Reagan's Economic Policy Advisory Board. He was also a consultant to Secretary of the Treasury William Simon, Margaret Thatcher, and others. The Laffer Curve, depicting the relationship between tax rates and tax revenue, is attributed to Arthur Laffer, though he never claimed to have invented it.

Gary Becker went to Princeton and the University of Chicago. He won the Nobel Memorial Prize in Economic Sciences in 1992 and the Presidential Medal of Freedom in 2007. He was considered one of the most important social scientists in America.

The other guy in the group was Merton Miller, from Boston. He graduated Harvard and earned his PhD in economics from Johns Hopkins. He also won the Nobel Prize in Economic Sciences in 1990.

Because of Jerry, I'd have all these guys over to the house, and we'd have dinner and talk about world events and the world economy. We'd talk about what various policies and wage and price controls meant, and we'd discuss laws being passed and how all of that was going to filter down into society. I never would have gained that experience and learned what I did if it wasn't for Gould, and I am eternally grateful to him for it.

30

THE SHEIKH OF ABU DHABI

Around 1981 to 1982, Randy Kreiling was living in Switzerland after his divorce from Helen Hunt, daughter of H. L. Hunt. One night, he was in a seedy Geneva strip club, where all the Arabs and every con artist in the world would go. It was there that Randy met a Pakistani who was working for Sheikh Zayed bin Sultan Al-Nahyan of Abu Dhabi. The Pakistani told Randy that Abu Dhabi wanted to corner the copper market. A bit later Randy called me to tell me he was coming to New York. He brought the Arabs with him and we met at my apartment in the old Mayfair Regent Hotel. The Arabs were all in their long robes and head scarves, and it was quite a picture. We brought out a blackboard so Randy could explain how the deal would work.

"What are you going to do with the copper?" I asked them. They said they were going to ship it out of Seattle, where most of it is, and send it to Abu Dhabi and put it in the desert where it's dry and it wouldn't corrode. This was all their idea, it's what they wanted to do, but I was thinking that squeezing copper was . . . well, it had already been done with the Hunts' silver squeeze, and it wasn't likely to be pulled off again. And then there were the shipping costs, my gosh. I don't know how they thought they were going to make money on this trade. "God bless," I said.

We took them down to Le Cirque, the restaurant in the hotel in those days, for dinner on Sunday night. It was Randy, me, and six Emiratis, and the waiter was preparing pheasant for us tableside in a frying pan with a long handle sticking out from the cart. A guy at a table near ours was drunker than hell and obviously had a prostitute with him. When he got up to leave, he passed out backwards over our cart. His body hit the handle on our skillet, the cart fell over, and the bird in the pan flew up into the air. It was a real sideshow. Then one of Emiratis looked at me and said, "Real classy place."

The sheikh's people went ahead and bought hundreds of thousands of copper contracts, which resulted in tons of business for us. They were taking delivery of the copper but eventually ran out of money because the sheikh decided he wasn't going to give them any more. So they got the copper, but they lost $100 million.

Not too long after, the sheikh sued Refco for $100 million. Then the State Department, FBI, and CIA all came to see me. They told me I had defrauded the sheikh and that they were going to bring the full force of the American government down on me unless I gave the sheikh his money back. I told them that I didn't take his fucking money, the marketplace took it, and that the sheikh's guys made a bad decision. I hadn't traded and I owed him nothing. I traded cattle and corn; I never traded copper or silver. They were welcome to look at my books and see for themselves. There was no way they could accuse me.

I was shocked that my own government seemed to be on the sheikh's side and against me. It was like they hadn't even bothered to learn the facts. They each came around a couple times and threatened me, not with death or anything, but by saying things like, "You're going to settle because we're looking out for him and not you." They made it clear to me that I was either going to give the sheikh his $100 million or they were going to make life tough for me.

I got a hold of some British lawyers out of London and told them we needed to meet with the sheikh. They set it up and off we went to Abu Dhabi.

We went to meet the sheikh on a Monday, but we didn't actually get to see him until Wednesday or Thursday. While we were waiting, we learned all the things we were supposed to do when meeting the sheikh, like properly greeting him by saying *Assalamu alaikum*, only shaking hands or giving our business cards with our right hands, and never showing the bottom of our shoes when we were sitting there, because it's insulting. While we were waiting for him, we noticed falcons sitting on the backs of chairs, shitting all over the lobby, and little Filipino women scrubbing falcon shit off the floor with toothbrushes. When it was finally our turn, we were taken into a square room with banquette seating all the way around where the sheikh met his people one day a week and heard their grievances.

When it was our time to talk, we told him through his interpreters that we didn't advise his people, we didn't solicit his people, and that we wouldn't even know where to find the people who worked for him. "You came to us to trade copper," I said. "You lost money and we're very sorry, but we did not take the money. It was the bad judgment of your advisors. They lost the money in the marketplace. We didn't advise you, and other than charge you commission for trading, we did nothing. As a matter of fact, we don't even do research on copper because that's not our area. We are both victims here. You lost money, and I'm getting sued for $100 million."

The sheikh turned to one of his advisors, who was kind of his Alan Greenspan at the time, and instructed him to have dinner with us. The advisor was from Abu Dhabi but he was Harvard educated and a smart guy. He spent the entire evening with us. He told us he had two daughters and that he wanted to get them out of Abu Dhabi and for them to be educated in the West. Tone Grant, who was Refco's General Counsel and who was with me at the meeting, had graduated from Andover and Yale. He and the advisor talked about getting his girls into American schools.

I had nothing to lose at this point except $100 million, so I decided to hustle him. "Look," I said. "We'd love to get your Abu Dhabi Investment Authorities Trust Account business."

Pause.

"If we can settle this lawsuit then we'll talk about it," the advisor said.

They dropped the lawsuit and we ended up getting about a quarter of the Abu Dhabi Investment Trust Account, which was worth billions of dollars. We went from a disaster to a home run. That advisor came to see us a few times in the US and he was a hell of a nice guy. He also wanted to get out of Abu Dhabi. I'm not sure what happened to him or if he ever got his girls into schools in the West, but I hope he did well.

31

DAVOS AND THE BROWN BAGS

The first time I went to Davos was in the early 1980s. A Swiss guy, Klaus Schwab, an engineer and economist who taught at the University of Geneva, started Davos in 1971.

Davos was originally called the European Management Forum, and Schwab invited about four hundred of the top European CEOs from thirty-one countries to come talk about competing in global markets. He wanted to introduce these people to the American style of business management. George Pierce Baker, who was then the dean of the Harvard Business School, was the symposium's first chairman. After a few years they expanded to political and social issues, and the conference grew from there. They made it an exclusive membership in 1977, and in 1987, they changed the name to the World Economic Forum. Everyone calls it Davos because it's held in Davos, Switzerland.

The first time I went, Jerry Gould was going to be one of the speakers and he asked me to tag along. He attends for free and so does Mert Miller; I paid $10,000. Now it's $100,000. At the time, there were maybe a thousand people attending and I only knew two guys.

"We need to make our contacts the first night," Jerry told me once we arrived.

"But I don't know anybody," I said.

"Here's how you do it," he said. He called Lou Dobbs, the television personality and author, and told him we were having dinner at seven that night. Then he dropped some names that Dobbs would find interesting. Dobbs said, "Okay, I'm there." Then Jerry called up the people whose names he had just dropped to Dobbs and told them Lou Dobbs was going to be there. They all came. We filled the room up with a lot of big guys who were also going to be speakers at the event. We did this every year for the first three years and the dinner parties got bigger and bigger, and other than the food, it didn't cost us anything. After every dinner you'd meet more people, so that during the day everyone was saying hi.

One year I was driving a rented Audi up the hill to go to Davos. I was pissed because they hadn't given me a Mercedes, but as I got up the hill I saw all these Mercedes that had slid off the road into snow banks, and that Audi just kept going! It was the best car ever. That same year we had dinner with the beautiful Gahl Burt, who had been President Reagan's Social Secretary. She was married to Richard Burt, who was the US ambassador to Germany. We had hung out with them before and had taken them shooting at Biddick. As I was chatting with Gahl, Karl Otto Pöhl asked if anyone wanted to go skiing the next morning. Now this guy was the head of Bundesbank, the central bank of Germany. Hell yes, I wanted to go skiing with him.

"What time?" Pöhl asked.

"9:30?" I said.

"Great."

Now keep in mind nobody at Davos really knew who I was or anything about me at the time. After we skied, I dropped Pöhl off and headed out to the event later that night. When I walked in, I spotted him across the room. He had about thirty guys around him, but when he saw me, he excused himself and rushed over. He wanted to know what time we were going skiing again in the morning. From that moment on it was like I was some kind of celebrity in Davos. "Tom, how you doing?" and "Tom, do you have time for a cup of coffee?" That was my best day at Davos, and from that day forward I was the guy.

★★★

Sometime in the late 1980s or early '90s, I traveled to Zurich to see Gary Steckler, who headed our office there. He was earning $200,000 to $300,000 a month in commissions, and I wanted to know how he was doing it.

"We do it the old-fashioned way," he said.

"How's that?"

"With brown bags."

"What?"

"The broker gives me his business, and every month I take a brown bag with cash in it and give him a rebate."

"You're kidding me!"

"No."

"Are you telling me that these guys who work for HSBC and UBS are taking cash back?"

"Yes!"

Astonished, I traveled to Paris to talk to Serge and found out they were doing the same thing in Paris.

"How are you getting Société Générale, the biggest bank in France, to pay us $300,000 a month in commission?" I asked. "How do you do this?"

"The brown bag," Serge said.

"What? You give each one of those fucking brokers a brown bag too?" I asked.

"Yes."

It was like walking into Citibank and handing money to all the tellers. Outrageous. As far as I knew, that sort of brown bagging did not happen in the States.

32

MY MOTHER AND POP

In 1983, Pop and Mother moved to Palm Beach permanently when I gave them my house on Tarpon Island. They loved it there and went out almost every night for every benefit party for every disease there was.

When Pop left Sioux City, he donated his house to Briar Cliff University, and it became an IRS hassle for him. No good deed goes unpunished. He was a practicing Jew, but he gave the house and grounds to a Catholic university because he was a friend of the head of the school. He had paid $250,000 for the house, and that's exactly what he wrote off, $250,000. He ended up spending $50,000 for lawyers and three years fighting the IRS over it. I had to laugh because it was so absurd, but he won in the end.

Pop was crazy about my mother, and she was crazy about him. He depended on her so much that if she was ten feet away, or upstairs in bed, or in the shower and he called for her, he expected her to answer immediately. When he was in his office at home in Palm Beach, he wanted her right next to him. And there she'd be, in a little room off his office where they kept the printer and stationery, smoking her cigarettes. And look what having him did for her life: she never had to worry about money again, and she had a good father for her son. It was nice for me to see.

My mother died of lung cancer in 1987. Pop took it very hard. He always thought he would die first because he was twenty-five years older than she was. When she went to Sloan Kettering in the last stages of the disease, she looked at him and said, "Ray, it's time. I'm ready. Push the morphine drip and let's get on with it." Her death devastated Pop, just killed him, and Frannie, too. Frannie loved my mother as much as she loved her own mom. Those two could talk and smoke cigarettes all night long. I think it was a big deal for my mother being a single parent. As she was dying she told me that she was scared at times in her life. I think that when she first got pregnant she thought about getting an abortion but decided against it. She mentioned to me in passing that because of her great success with me, she had become pro-life. The funeral was held at the First Baptist Church in Hawarden and the burial in Grace Hill Cemetery, surrounded by cornfields.

Years later, Pop married Maria Ponton who was Argentinean, pretty, nice, and sweet as sugar. Her son is Dan Ponton who owns, among other things, the Club Colette, a private supper club in Palm Beach. Pop's daughter, Lisette, and her son, Bradley, did not want Pop to remarry. I told Pop marrying Maria was the right thing to do.

"But I promised your mother. . . ." Pop said.

"Pop, she would tell you the same thing," I said. "You have to marry her so that she'll get your inheritance tax-free. What are you thinking? You've already given your grandkids and everybody money. Lisette doesn't need money, she's got a fifty-million-dollar house in Malibu and she married well. But Maria needs the money, so marry her and give her the fucking money." So he did marry her, and Lisette and Bradley were both pissed at me. Pop and Maria stayed married until he died in 2004, at ninety-one. I still talk to Maria a couple of times a year.

33

HIDING FROM TOM
by Kim Sherman

I met Tom when I interviewed to become his secretary in January 1987. I had worked for a couple of years as a flight attendant, but that didn't train me to do much except serve drinks in turbulence. I wanted to go back to school at night, and I needed a day job where I didn't have to think a whole lot.

All I knew about the Refco job was that it paid up to $25,000 a year. That's all I cared about. My interview wasn't very long, and he didn't say much. The extent of the job description was that he needed someone outside his office to do "stuff," and offered me the job for $15,000. That should have been a big-ass red flag right there. He eventually came up to $25,000, but you would have thought he had given me a body part. I didn't know anything about Tom or his business and didn't care. I just needed the paycheck.

When I started working for Tom, I thought he was fine. He was a tall guy in a nice office in the Loop. He could have been selling hemorrhoid cream. I didn't care. My office was outside of his office. Frannie had decorated it, and it was beautiful. But there was nothing on my desk except a telephone, not even a Rolodex. I had no idea what to do. There was no manual and no one ever came to talk to me and tell me what I should be doing. Nothing. In hindsight, I think people avoided that area because who wanted to be around him?

On my first day there, Tom yelled something about bacon. What did that mean? Was I supposed to get his breakfast? Was I supposed to cook it? What?

"Did you want breakfast?" I asked.

"Damnit, I'll get it myself," he snapped. He started pounding numbers on the phone. He was calling Louis Bacon! Did I know Louis Bacon? I didn't know Louis Bacon. This was an alternate universe to me. I didn't know any of this stuff and he was terrifying. He would scream these things out as he went from zero to sixty in about a nanosecond, then go back to zero. He just kept yelling for these people. I had the phone list, but that was no help when he yelled, "Get Dude down here!" Dude wasn't on the phone list.

"Who is that?" I asked him.

"Damnit, I'll get him myself!!"

Well, I thought, *I'm fucked.*

It was only the $25,000 that kept me grounded. Tom was very off-putting. There was nothing charming about him. "You need to go to my house," he stated. Okay, that's unusual. I'd never worked for anyone who told me I had to go to his house. He told me that I needed to meet his wife and the household staff because I would be working with them, too. He did a lot of his business entertaining at home.

My husband and I lived in a crappy apartment on Halsted Street, near Lincoln Park. The next day this guy pulled up in a limousine—I don't know what I was expecting, but I got in the front seat. I'd never been in a limousine before. I didn't know what to do.

We drove up to Lake Forest and went in through the gates to this very nice house. Well, that turned out to be the gatehouse, where the help lived. We pulled up to the main house and it was gorgeous, understated, elegant. Steve, the driver, let me off at the front door and the butler opened it. Of course, why not? Ian, the butler, who had an English accent, walked me inside. It was like walking through a magazine. I met Lois, Frannie's personal secretary, and she kept apologizing that I wasn't able to see the grounds. I thought I had seen the grounds when we first came in, and that they were very nice. What I hadn't seen was the other thirty acres, which was big even by Lake Forest standards. I met Frannie for the first time that day and she was lovely. She was so attractive, so statuesque, and so confident. She also had a great sense of humor.

So I was working for this crazy guy, and going through this gorgeous mansion, and I felt like the biggest rube in the world. I was scared to death of Tom, but these people were all friendly, albeit somewhat aloof. We got back into the limo and went to the office. That was early on and I hadn't realized yet what I was getting myself into. I thought that I would work for some guy, type some letters, finish my undergraduate work, and get on with my life. It turned out to be something very, very different. This was a world of second and third homes and private jets. I didn't know what a tail number was. "Get me the fucking tail number!" he would shout. What is that? A prostitute's ass? It was all new to me.

The year 1987 turned out to be very interesting. I started to settle in, but I was afraid to ask Tom for anything because he yelled all the time. He'd yell, "Get me some lunch." I was afraid to ask him for money, so I spent several weeks buying the guy lunch. My lunch was an apple I brought from home because I needed my cash for his lunch. Sometimes I would hide under the conference room table just to get away from him. He would be yelling, "Sherman!" Then he would go pound on the women's restroom door. "Sherman!" People didn't seem to think that the CEO pounding on the ladies room door was weird.

One day he said, "You need to plan a Christmas party." He wanted to have it at the Field Museum of Natural History. I'm thinking, *Are you talking about the big building with the dinosaurs in it?* I didn't know you could have a party there. By this time, I was having nightmares about drowning while a phone was ringing and I couldn't get to it. Now I had to plan a party at a dinosaur palace. This should be good.

What was very sad about that year was Tom's mother's illness and death. I would have loved to have met this woman because I think she was the heart of everything for Tom. It didn't sink in at the time, perhaps because I was hiding under the conference room table, that he had all the money in the world, and he couldn't do anything for the person who mattered most to him. After Evelyn passed away, Tom asked me, in a very polite tone, if I would go to Iowa to help coordinate the funeral service. It was Labor Day Weekend, and I said, "Absolutely."

Hawarden is in the middle of nowhere. Tom was distraught, so I bought my own ticket to Sioux City. My flight ended up being canceled and they re-routed me through St. Louis, but I couldn't get to Hawarden that night and I was really pressed for time.

Fortunately, by then I was beginning to understand these people who traveled by private plane. So I chartered a flight and charged it to my credit card. All I could think was, *Oh my God, if I don't get to Hawarden, Dittmer's going to kill me. When I tell my husband that I chartered a plane, he's going to kill me.* When I got to Sioux City, I rented a car, again on my credit card. I realized I didn't have anything to wear to the funeral so I bought a skirt and sweater. Finally, I got to Hawarden, and somehow it all came together.

I went to work the next day and Tom said, "Thank you. You gave up your holiday. I want to send you and your husband somewhere and I'll pay for it."

"Oh, I can't do that. This was your mom's funeral. It's not necessary, but thank you," I said. I'm an idiot.

"Well," Tom said, "you talk to your husband. Tell him I want to do this."

I went home and I told my husband. "Tell him yes, before he changes his mind," my husband said. My husband, by then, had a sense of Tom's attention span.

I go to work the next day and tell Tom that we'd love to go somewhere.

"Where do you want to go? London, Paris, Rome?" Tom asked.

Again, it was that alternate universe where I thought he was offering a nice hotel in Chicago or New York. I was blown away. He really did want to do something nice for me, and it meant a lot to him.

We went to London and we were taken around town in a Rolls Royce. We had sixth row center seats for *Phantom of the Opera*, which had just opened. It was an amazing trip and it was Tom's grand way of saying thank you. It was wonderful. This really gave me an opportunity to see his humanity, his generosity, and his heart.

I finally got the nerve up to see Tom's financial guy and get reimbursed for the plane tickets, the chartered plane, and the rental car. All I had to do was ask the right person. Tom just didn't deal with those things himself.

When the time came for the Christmas party at the Field Museum, I was able to pull it off and it went well. All I can say is, thank God Tom was in Aspen when the bills came in. I didn't know at the time that I could just say to him, "You want a grand party? Well, you have to fucking pay for it!" After working for Tom that first year, I got stronger. I knew what I had to do on the job and how to deal with him. He was crazy, but he was so fucking funny! I did finally get used to him.

34

PROVIDENCE ST. MEL

My mother's family, the Robertsons, came from around Green-ville, Kentucky. They were prosperous farmers, but the Civil War wiped them out. They sold their land, which is now Fort Campbell, and moved to the Midwest.

After my mother died, I started thinking about what was important in life. I had long been concerned about the conditions in the black community and I decided to take a couple of night courses at Lake Forest College to study slavery, to understand the evolution of poverty and the economic challenges of the black community.

Kim Sherman was my secretary at the time and I just loved her. "Kim," I said, "find me the inner city schools that we can help out and give money to." I had gone to public schools myself and so did my kids until they reached high school. Kim visited some public schools and found out that because of the janitors' union rules, schools were closed every day at two o'clock. I told Kim, "I'm not doing public schools. Let's find another school."

Two or three weeks later Kim came back and said, "I've found it. It's a little private school on the West Side run by a guy named Paul Adams." I had an apartment in downtown Chicago and I invited Paul there for dinner. I liked him the minute we met. We ate, drank, and it felt like we were brothers. Like me, Paul was raised by a single mother who could be tough on him. Both of our mothers had the same philosophy: You are going to do what's right.

"I'm not sure," I told him, "but I think your mother and my mother might have been related."

When Paul was fourteen years old, Martin Luther King, Jr. came to visit his school, and Paul met him. Paul later participated in the Montgomery bus boycott in 1955 and was a part of the Civil Rights sit-ins and marches while he was attending Alabama State University. A photo of him taken during the Selma to Montgomery marches appeared in *Life* magazine. He was arrested at a protest and kicked out of college for a year, but he returned and graduated eventually. Not long afterward he moved to Chicago.

At Providence St. Mel, Paul was principal, teacher, maintenance man, and bus driver. He lived above the school in the attic with a cot and a hot plate. "That's good," I said. "You just go down the stairs and you're at work." He told me the school had a budget of about $900,000 a year, and he was paid out of whatever was left. It might have been $900 or $9,000. This guy was walking the walk.

I went to the school and saw that it was all black kids and was located in one of the most violent neighborhoods in America. The nearby houses were all government projects and the colors on the buildings told you which gangs controlled the territory. If you were a Red, you walked all the way around that street so you didn't have to go through the Yellow because if you did, you'd get killed.

"That's why I have a gun and a baseball bat," Paul told me. "I know who the gangbangers are and they don't come to my school because

I'm head of my gang, and they're head of theirs, and the twain should not meet."

Paul would do anything he could to raise money for the school—fish fries, bingo games, bake sales, you name it. At one time they even had a McDonald's in the basement of the school, but they had to close it because it kept getting robbed. I asked Paul to give me a list of things that he needed to do and we'd go from there. I gave him some money to fund scholarships, and I hired Betty Graham as the development director. She was part of a big-time Chicago family, and I paid her $200,000 out of my own pocket—plus a bonus—to help raise money to get the school in shape. She was fabulous and within six months she had raised $3 million. From there it went to $7 million and up.

About two years after I got involved with the school, I told Paul that every year my son and daughter went overseas to learn something new. I suggested that his top students should do the same thing. We organized the Summer Opportunity of a Lifetime; they called it SOAL, and made plans to send thirty or forty kids overseas for summer school. We also sent them to great East Coast schools like Exeter and Andover.

When time came for the first summer trip, the kids' parents asked Paul how they were going to get to the airport. Paul said, "I don't know. I'm not going to take them." Paul didn't believe in doing everything for everybody, and the parents figured out how to get their kids to the airport. You should have seen the neighborhood when the children came home. There were banners strung across the streets, *Welcome Home* with the kids' names. It was a big celebration. It was great. For the first time in their lives, these kids had expectations they'd never dreamed of before.

We took them on other trips, too, like rafting in the Grand Canyon, kayaking on the Green River, and skiing in Aspen. I'd fill up my plane with kids and we'd take them out for a week. But for the students to be eligible for SOAL or the other trips, they had to have mostly As.

Paul handpicked the kids, and in addition to achieving good grades, they had to exhibit leadership qualities.

Discipline is an important part of the school. When you walk into assembly, it is quiet. When Paul Adams walks onto the auditorium stage, you can hear a pin drop. The kids wear uniforms, and there is a strict behavioral code. No gang association, no graffiti, no stealing, no drugs, no gambling. Any of those things will get a kid expelled. One year the school was poised to win the state basketball championship. The star of the team, who went on to earn a college scholarship, had to have all Bs to play and he didn't have them. Easy decision. He wasn't playing. The kids and his parents went wild.

"Wait a second," Paul told them. "We're not here for basketball, we're here for education. He knew the rules. He's not playing." The team lost.

There was a copy of the school rules on the back of every student's notebook so that if they ever got confused, all they had to do was turn over their notebook and read the rules.

Soon Providence St. Mel became popular and all the kids in that bad part of town wanted to go there.

After a couple of years, the school had an annual budget of $7 million. Half of the kids were on full scholarship and half paid $1,000 a year. There were fifty-five teachers, mostly white, and they were not earning as much as public school teachers made at the time. They got health insurance, but no retirement benefits. What they got in the trade-off was personal safety and respect. At Providence St. Mel the teacher teaches and is highly respected. Teachers never got called "Teach" except once, because that kid would be gone in minutes. Period.

Since PSM began, 100 percent of every graduating class has been accepted to college. Not 100 percent have been able to attend, for financial or other reasons, but 100 percent have been accepted. But that's not the impressive news. What's impressive is that 77 percent of them graduate from college in four years. The national average is less than half that. Out of each graduating class, 70 percent of them go to first-tier schools or better. Better! We're talking MIT, Yale, Stanford, and Harvard. These kids are prepared to succeed.

The first time we took students to Andover—we went because my daughter Alexis was going to school there—they had what they called the MS Squared math program. Andover started it back in 1977 to help underserved and inner-city kids learn math and science. It's an intense few weeks where they compress a year's worth of math and science into a few weeks' time and give the kids a taste of what it's like to be in college. The students come away skilled and confident in their abilities. They had the same program at Exeter, with sixteen places available. Four were PSM students. Paul went to visit and saw the black kids were out of control. Not Paul's kids, but the others, doing whatever they wanted. Meanwhile, the white kids were well-behaved and working away.

Paul pulled the person in charge aside. "I resent the fact that you don't have the same rules for the black kids," he said, "and if you can't change it, I'm taking my kids back home." He knew the teachers thought they were being kind, but he saw it as a double standard. Paul called it double racism. "So," Paul said, "you want them to graduate, think they're okay, and then when they're twenty years old find out that they don't measure up. I want them to know now. Either they follow the same rules and take the same tests, or we're not doing it. I want them to learn to compete today." That's Paul Adams.

Educating these kids in math and science is important, but if they're going to go to prestigious schools and do important work, they also have to know how to navigate a world very different from the one they grew up in. Two or three times a year Development Director Betty Graham would take a group of ten or so young guys to dinner. We'd buy them suits and ties, and Betty would teach them how to hold a knife and fork properly, how to eat in a restaurant, and generally how to behave as gentlemen. Then I would take that same group to the Economic Club of Chicago, where I was a member. The club meets several times a year to hear a big-name speaker and to have dinner, and the boys knew how to handle themselves in that environment.

In 1996 the school hired Jeanette Butala as the Lower School Director, and the next year she became assistant principal. Within three years, test scores were up 35 percent. An Italian spitfire and a tough-love kind of person, Jeanette had worked in the public schools as a special education teacher for seventeen years. She became principal in 2000 and Paul became president. She is an incredible woman who knows how to get things done.

We also had an amazing board of directors. One of the people I recruited to be on the board was Stedman Graham, Oprah Winfrey's partner. Frannie and I saw Oprah and Stedman often in those days. They would come to dinner at our house every other month or so. We traveled together occasionally and and we were always in touch.

In 1993, we held a big fund-raising dinner for the school at the Hyatt Regency. Board members Karen Pritzker and Stedman introduced Oprah as the special guest. It was really cute. She got up on the stage holding a shoebox and said that she wanted to clean out her shoe closet and give the profits to Providence St. Mel. So she held a sale at Harpo Studios and charged $10 for shoes and $5 for sneakers. It came to more than $600. She handed Paul Adams a little box presumably with the check. That was nice but it didn't exactly set off fireworks. Then she said, "I thought I had more shoes than that." Paul Adams opened the box and pulled out another check for $1 million. That was Oprah.

President Reagan visited the school twice. On his second visit in 1983, he said PSM was a shining light and a model for the nation's schools to emulate. In 2009 a documentary called *The Providence Effect* was released and was awarded Most Socially Engaging Feature at the

Eugene International Film Festival. The kids educated at Providence
St. Mel owe everything to Paul and Jeanette.

Paul Adams: My Brother Tom

In 1971 I began work at Providence St. Mel, a coed Catholic
high school on the West Side of Chicago. I started as director
of guidance, and the next year I became principal. That's when
we set up strict rules against gangs, drugs, graffiti, fighting, and
so on. Any of those would be grounds for expulsion. It was
tough, but we were making headway. Then in 1978 the arch-
diocese decided to close the school. I met with Sister Loretta
Schafer, the Superior General of the Sisters of Providence, and
asked her if I could lease the school building. She said no, but
that she would sell it to me. My heart sank. I told her that I
didn't have any money, and she said, "Well, you'll find it." It
was with that faith that I am now able to talk about this. We
eventually did buy the building for a very modest amount.

I met Tom in 1989 through Dren Geer, who was at that time
headmaster at Francis Parker, a private school in Chicago. He
called me to say that there was a young man looking for a char-
ity to get involved with. A few months went by and I got a call
from Kim Sherman, Tom's "chief of staff." She said that she
would like to come visit the school. "But," she said, "that
doesn't mean we're going to give you the money." We had a lot
of people visit us, so that didn't mean anything to me.

Kim came and spent the day with us, and then Tom came
out and spent three or four hours. He thought it was the most
wonderful place. "By the way," he said to me, "I'm going to
have a little party for you."

I thought we would just go somewhere and have a few
drinks, but he rented out the Chicago Historical Society. Oh

my God, guest speakers and a five-course meal, and I was thinking *Where did this man come from?* and *We need to get this man on the board.* I approached him and he said, "Hell, no. Someone might sue me."

But he finally succumbed, and once he was on the board, he wanted to take over. And he did take over. He took a boulder off my shoulders and allowed me to breathe as an administrator. The long and the short of it was that Tom Dittmer saved this school. He was able to pull together the right people in Chicago and get the financing for the school. He changed the board of trustees into a fund-raising group. I think he was chairman of the board for about ten years, and this institution is better for it.

Tom started the Bright Nights program, which paid a student's tuition except for $50 a month that the parents paid. He bought a bus for the school so that the kids could be picked up and get here safely. He paid for tutors. He was unbelievable. The SOAL program he started still operates. Tom would literally take kids all over the world—to Africa, Asia, France, Switzerland, Spain, everywhere. That program has been an equalizer in many ways. By taking these kids from the inner city and putting them into areas that they would never have had opportunities to visit, they find out that they can be competitive. He sent two girls to France one year, and they had spent time with kids going to Stanford. They came back and said, "We want to go to Stanford." They both went to Stanford and graduated.

Tom and Frannie bought the property across the street from the school and renovated the house from the ground up. Tom brought in his contractor, landscaper, and the interior designer David Easton. Frannie came down and picked out the furniture, and boy, talk about a turnkey. All we had to do was to go to Wal-Mart and pick up the food for the first night we spent there. That's where we lived and where we hold special events and board functions. We also bought up properties in the neighborhood because Tom thought that would be a good deal for the school. We bought about thirty empty lots in the area and now own a group of houses comprising twenty-four units for people of low income.

Tom and I became friends as soon as we met. Here was this man with a tremendous amount of money talking to someone who didn't have that kind of money and treating him with dignity and respect. Everywhere he goes and spends any time, he tries to find something to do to help someone else. That's Tom.

Jeanette Butala: Just Get It Done

The same year I was made assistant principal, Principal Paul Adams chose not to renew contracts for six of our teachers. There was an uproar, and forty-eight staff members quit. It was summer, and Tom was away with our SOAL students at an Oxbridge Academic Program. Paul was out on the speaking circuit, leaving me with forty-eight teachers and staff to hire in less than three months.

I did it. That fall, at the first board meeting, instead of Tom saying, "Wow, great job," he said, "So, how many kids are going to Ivy Leagues this year?" I was thinking, *Are you kidding me?*

Tom set the bar high and was fiercely focused on results. For someone who wasn't an educator, he understood well that the key for African American kids in the hood was to get into great colleges, period. He didn't give a damn how, he just wanted it done.

At that point I'd been in urban education for seventeen years at seven different schools. Most of my supervisors had been African American, but none were as gifted as Paul Adams. He spoke such pure language, like he would tell the students not to wear red shoes to a job interview or they wouldn't get the job. Other administrators I had been around wouldn't say things like that because they feared it would be interpreted as racist. Being at Providence St. Mel was so gratifying for me because I had the combination of an incredible African American visionary and Tom Dittmer.

In board meetings Tom took no prisoners and he would say almost anything. I remember one board meeting when somebody said something Tom didn't like, he told him to sit the bleep down. Only he didn't say bleep. I really didn't want that to happen to me, so every time I went to a board meeting I was totally over-prepared.

"How long is this going to take?" Tom asked. Then while I was thinking about how to condense it, he said, "Just give us the bad news."

"Okay," I said, "how long do I have?"

"Three minutes," he said.

I said, "I will do my best to get these kids into great colleges, but I need a three-to-five-year plan."

"You can't have five," Tom said, "but you can have three."

The class of 2001 was the first in which half of the students were accepted into first-tier and Ivy League schools. At the next board meeting, I made a packet and sent it out to the board members ahead of time. Tom read every page and had questions for me. He was always interested in how I was putting things together.

Tom was a combination of charisma and drive and it was fun being around him. You wanted to please him and you didn't want him to embarrass you if you irritated him. The reason we stand today is because of two people: Sister Loretta Schafer, who sold the school to Paul; and Tom Dittmer, who raised the money to keep the school open. Today, our operating budget is $8 million. Our tuition revenue is only $2 million, so we have to raise $6 million a year. At least $4 million of that is still coming in from connections to Tom.

35

RACING WITH GAGS

Another guy who changed my life was Mike "Gags" Gagliardo. He was from Chicago and his dad owned Columbus Foods. Gags loved going fast. Even as a kid, he used to race the forklift around his dad's company. After his dad died, Gags and his sister Paulette took over the company, but Gags kept racing cars. He was also a good trader in cooking oil on the commodities market.

Not long after my mother died in 1987, Gags got my son Jason and me into racing cars with him. He had us go to Skip Barber Racing School in Sebring, Florida. We learned on Formula 4s driving 100-horsepower cars that weighed maybe 900 pounds. We learned skid control, how to corner, everything you needed to know on the racetrack.

We started racing with Gags and Refco president Tone Grant. At first we drove regular BMW 325is, but then we moved up to GT3 Porsches. We bought two Porsches and a big semitruck. We stored the cars one on top of the other in half the truck and used the other half for sleeping and watching films of our races. The films came from cameras mounted in the cars. They had a view out the front wind-shield and recorded braking, gas, and speed.

I hated that camera. One day I was practicing around the track on "the Glen," the Watkins Glen racetrack in western New York. I was on the radio headset and the guy in my ear was saying, "You've got to go in pulling at least 4,000 rpm in third gear, and when you hit the apex, you've got to be at 5,000 rpm. At the rollout after the turn you've got to be doing 7,000."

"Got it," I said.

"How's it going?" he asked me.

I said, "I'm on the numbers. I've got 'em."

"Are you hitting the apex?" he asks.

"Nailing it!"

When I finished, I went into the truck to watch the film. I thought I was turning at least 4,000 rpm, but the camera showed I was only doing 2,000. When I hit the apex maybe I got up to 3,500 but not the 5,000 I was supposed to do. On the rollout, I may have gotten all the way to 6,000, but I missed the apex by a mile. It was terrible. That camera didn't lie.

Jason, Gags, Tone, and I ended up racing together for seven years at a lot of different tracks. Jason got to be really good at it. We quit because it was so damn expensive, and I was getting too old.

Gags was killed in May 2001, forty-six years old, in an accident during his first race of the Sports Car Club of America's Trans Am Series in Ontario. He died before they even got him to the hospital. He was a complete gearhead and loved everything about racing and cars. What a great guy.

36

FISHING WITH DAD
by Jason Dittmer

Let's be honest, when you're a twenty-year-old kid flying around in a private plane and racing cars with your dad, you're just the coolest kid on the planet. I was not living in the real world by any means, but Dad was so proud of me, and it was so much fun!

Fishing, on the other hand, wasn't Dad's thing. He hated fishing, but I loved it and he would take me. He'd get seasick and throw up, but he would do it. One time he had a friend with a ranch in Gunnison, Colorado, and he asked me if I wanted to go there and go fishing. Of course I wanted to go! We flew from Aspen over to Gunnison and there we were fishing with my dad who was sitting nearby, not fishing. Those trout were huge, and pretty soon I caught one. I couldn't have been more than ten or eleven years old, and I was having a heck of a time trying to reel that fish in. It was just immense. My dad perked up and he became seriously invested in getting this fish in, but it was literally too big to pull to shore. So, my dad, in chinos,

Oxford shirt and loafers, jumped into the lake, grabbed this fish, and threw it up onto the bank. He wanted me to have that fish and that's what was going to happen. That was the kind of thing my dad would do.

37

STUDS TERKEL

O ne day I got a phone call. "Tom Dittmer?" the guy asked. "Yes sir," I said.

"This is Studs Terkel."

"Yeah, and I'm the Queen of England," I quipped.

Studs Terkel was a legend in Chicago. He had been the voice of Chicago radio and appeared frequently on television. An outspoken free spirit, he was also an historian, author, and Pulitzer Prize winner. His 1967 book *Division Street: America* had been one of his bestsellers. Division Street in Chicago is one long street where you can go all the way from expensive Lake Shore Drive to the gangbanger neighborhoods, effectively spanning the socioeconomic spectrum of America.

"No, no," he said. "Really, I'm Studs Terkel."

"Sure you are," I said. I was thinking, *I'm in the commodities business, so why would Studs Terkel be calling me?*

"I'm doing research for a book and I'd like to talk to you."

"Are you really Studs Terkel? *Division Street: America*?" I asked.

It was Studs Terkel. I told him he couldn't use my name but that I'd love to talk to him, and he came to the office. He was a piece of work, very funny, and a real character. We talked about Chicago and what was going to happen to the commodities business. I told him that I didn't think it had a long-term future because I had always thought of it as a hot dog stand. The margins were thin, and if you gave away too much pickle or mustard you didn't make any money. Commodities are different from stocks because if you buy a stock, no one has to lose money for you to make money. In commodities, if you win, the guy who sells it to you loses, so there's always a loser.

Every customer who has a good trade, it's his idea; and every customer who has a losing trade, it's the broker's idea. When I started in the commodities business, the commissions were $40. Today they're three cents. Computers do all the trading now and the business I knew is gone. I used to think we'd go to virtual reality, where you could be anywhere in the world and you could trade like you were standing in the pit. But nope, computers took over after all.

I also told Studs that I thought that the commodities exchanges were monopolies and different from stock exchanges. You can trade IBM stock in fourteen exchanges around the world, but you can only trade soybeans in Chicago. Exchanges have the monopoly and they can raise prices. But as a clearinghouse, you have to compete with other firms so you don't want to raise prices.

Over the years I've talked to several authors about Chicago and the commodities business, but never on the record because I didn't want to call attention to myself. And now here I am writing my memoir. Go figure. What Studs and I talked about was all background for his book *Chicago*, which came out in 1986. It was a great little book about the city he loved. I love that city, too.

38

THE IRS AT HIGH NOON

From the late '80s to the early '90s, the IRS was after me with a vengeance. After the tax laws changed under Reagan in the '80s and taxable gains had to be paid in the same year they were made, I found myself with taxes due on $100 million in gains. I paid it. Some months later the IRS accused me of fraud. Now they wanted $300 million from me and accused me of making phony trades.

Here is why I love Chicago. Well, one of the reasons. And this is one of the best stories I can tell you about the kind of town it was back then. It was Sunday, August 27, 1989, and the headline on the front page of the *Chicago Tribune*'s Business section read, "US Probes Refco Chief's Investments." Basically saying, if the government is investigating, he must have done something. That miserable fuck Dittmer is finally going to go to jail for tax fraud. I was sitting at breakfast reading this and I was devastated. I was sure that everybody in town had read the news, that the kids read it, and that the families where my kids went to school all read it. Then the phone rang.

"Hi, Tom, this is Cindy Pritzker. May I speak to Frannie?"

I gave Frannie the phone and we both thought we knew why she was calling. We were about to be cut off from everybody and everything.

"Frannie," Cindy said, "I'm chair of the new Chicago Library opening and I'd like for you to be my cochair."

"Cindy, have you seen the papers?" Frannie asked.

"I have, that's why I'm calling. It's bullshit. To hell with 'em. I want you to be my cochair."

To this day, thinking about that phone call brings tears to my eyes. In essence, Cindy was saying, I don't give a shit, they're wrong and you're great, and you're going to be my cochair. The next day my face appeared on the front page of the *Wall Street Journal*. I was as good as guilty. But to friends in Chicago, we were okay. That's Chicago.

I hired Cono Namorato, a DC lawyer who had worked for Bobby Kennedy during the Jimmy Hoffa trial. He actually had more respect for Hoffa than for Kennedy. He said that if Hoffa said something, you could bank on it. If Bobby said something, you had no idea. Cono said that to win, I had to beat the IRS "a hundred to one." Anything less and with the rulebook in their favor, they'd prosecute me. Civil charges are one thing, but criminal charges are another. Then you pay serious attention.

The IRS claimed my cattle business, which at the time was still the biggest feedlot in the world, was a tax dodge. Fighting that took about six months, and they dropped it. But they then claimed that all those trades I made—me, not Refco—had to be fraudulent because I traded from my own account more than any grain company in the world. And I did. I was like a wild guy; I made brash moves that no one had ever made before. And forget innocent until proven guilty. I had to prove that I was innocent. So I had two exchequers from the Bank of England testify on my behalf. I reconciled my books with the books of every exchange I traded on in London, Chicago, and Singapore. There were an average of four million trades a year. Out of some twenty million trades, there was only one trade they couldn't match, and it was insignificant.

I appeared before the Justice Department three times. Again, me personally, not Refco. I got one hour to make my case, and then they got one hour. After all that I received a letter containing a couple lines saying that the criminal investigation had been canceled. That was it, after ten years and $17 million in legal fees. None of it should ever have happened in the first place. Everyone did the kinds of spreads and trades I was doing, and it was all perfectly legal. I was the only guy that got prosecuted.

Why me? My personal lawyer, Marshall Eisenberg, said I had more IRS audits than the Pritzkers, and they've got way more money than I. He told me someone had "dropped a dime on me." I tried to find out who it was through the Freedom of Information Act. Marshall warned me, "You do know who you're dealing with, right? Do you want to start this all over again? Don't fuck with them."

Doesn't matter now. I'm just happy I'm here.

39

SPANISH COWS AND OTHER COCKAMAMIE SCHEMES

Sometime in the mid-1990s, Paul Engler and I went to Santiago de Campostela, Spain, to meet with the minister of agriculture. They were going to loan us money, interest-free for twenty years, to buy cows. During those twenty years, we could sell the calves and keep the profit. At the end of the twenty years, we'd give them the cowherd. So, if we bought 200,000 cows with their money, at the end of the deal we would have to give them 200,000 cows. They wanted us to graze the cattle on the commons in every town. You know how many town commons there are in Spain? Thousands. It was millions of acres but they were scattered all over the country.

We told them it was conceivable, but that we were going to need a lot of pickup trucks and CB radios. Not possible, they said, because both had been declared illegal since the 1936 revolution. Pickups could have been used to transport guns and soldiers, and CB radios would give them a way to communicate. I don't know what the laws are today, but that was the case twenty years ago. But the coup de grâce was when we asked about their cowboys. Who would take care of the cows?

The minister looked at us and said, "Well, usually it's the grand-mother who lives with the guy who owns the cows."

We drove around looking at the commons and talking about the logis-tics of managing, say, 500 commons and 200,000 cows. Even though we were offered a staggering amount of money, we told them it couldn't be done. We needed trucks, radios, and cowboys, not grandmas.

The minister said, "But we're giving you the money."

"But it's impossible to manage," we told him.

I once flew down to the Dominican Republic with Eldon Jewel, a big hog farmer from Iowa whom I was in business with at the time. The Dominican government didn't have any money, but they wanted to trade us pigs for sugar. They wanted us to fly the piglets down in cargo planes. I got suspicious when they said we would have to give them the pigs before they would give us the sugar. We would get the sugar, they said, but they couldn't do it right away. I went home and did a little checking and decided the whole thing was a con. They were going to get the pigs and that was it. Once we delivered the pigs, what were we going to do? Chase them around and get them back?

Another time Engler and I were in Venezuela—again in the mid-1990s—looking at buying the old King Ranch down there. That's when we saw this giant rodent sitting on its haunches, a capybara. It was as big as a dog but it looked like a rat. They have really soft skin that the people down there use like leather. Capybaras can weigh up to forty-five pounds or more, and grow to be two feet high and four and a half feet long. While that thing was sitting there looking at us, a boa constrictor came up, killed it, and ate it right in front of us. Boom.

Maybe the goofiest was the time Engler and I went to Bulgaria. We were in the capital, Sofia, and we were talking cattle. Other than in Spain, everyone wanted us to finance everything. The Bulgarians would give us the land, but we would have to supply the money and the cattle.

We gave them a slideshow and showed them what it was going to look like. They were going to do feedlots, not ranching, so they'd need grain to feed the cattle. We told them that in Texas, we used thirty-five million bushels of corn a year. In those days, that was more corn than the US sold to Russia in a year.

"How much grain do you have?" we asked them.

"It's not quite that big," they said.

I told them that if they had to buy corn, they would be losing their edge. Normally we could build the feedlot at $100 to $200 a head—that's how you price feedlots. In Bulgaria, though, it would have been cheaper because the labor was basically free. But without the corn for feeding, the cattle conversation died there.

"How about financing a ski resort?" they asked us.

They actually have big mountains there, but Bulgaria wasn't exactly a big tourist destination. We passed.

40

FATAL TRADES
AND BACK TO CUBA

I had been trying to get Chris Parrott, one of Cook Grain's top trad-ers, to trade with us. This was in the 1990s. He didn't want to work with me because Willard Sparks was with us and Willard was an ex-Cook guy, too. Eventually Chris did clear with us, producing some $20 million a year in gross commissions, which meant he was taking home $8 to $10 million a year. One day he asked me to loan him some money. I forget why he said he needed it, although I remember his wife was a big spender. Anyway, I loaned him the money because he was such a huge producer, and I thought I'd get it back. He made his first payment to me about six months later, and made a joke about how he was probably the first guy ever to pay me back.

The next weekend Chris put a shotgun in his mouth and killed himself.

His Hungarian partner, Gabor Morvay, who used to work for the Hungarian Grain Company in Budapest, paid me a visit shortly there-after. He told me that Chris killed himself because he had been caught stealing from the Russians, siphoning monies from their trading accounts into his own pockets. Chris put the trades in his name, and they sent the checks to Chris directly. They never came through Refco. The thing I couldn't understand was, with the kind of money he was making, why did he need to steal? I told Gabor that I wasn't stealing from the Russians and that the checks had never come through Refco. A year or so later they found Gabor hanging by his neck underneath a bridge in Budapest. I'm guessing it was the Russians who did it.

It all reminded me of Roberto Calvi, the guy they called "God's banker" because he was chairman of Banco Ambrosiano and also banker to the Vatican. Ambrosiano went under, but a few months before, Calvi was arrested for sending millions of dollars out of the country illegally. They found him in 1982 hanging from Blackfriars Bridge in London.

Trading can be a rough business.

★★★

In the '90s I made another trip to Cuba, this time with Rick Kaplan, who was working at ABC then. During his CBS days as a producer in the 1970s, Rick had met and become friendly with Bill Clinton. I'm assuming there was some quasi-official Clinton government business that prompted Rick's visit, but he didn't tell me and I didn't ask. In any event I was allowed to fly us down in my Falcon 900.

The night before we were to have dinner with Castro, Rick and I had dinner with Ricardo Alarcón de Quesada. Alarcón was Cuba's permanent representative to the UN, minister of foreign affairs, then president of the National Assembly of People's Power. After Fidel and his brother, Raúl, he was the third most powerful guy in Cuba. Refco had already been doing the oil-for-sugar trade out of London, so he knew of us.

Alarcón came to dinner with us in Siboney, which used to be the Beverly Hills of Havana, with mansions, country clubs, and summer homes. After the revolution those buildings were repurposed into offices and embassies. Siboney was also the place where Castro and his men gathered before they attacked the Moncada Barracks in 1953, marking the start of the revolution.

The house we stayed in was beautiful, but the lawns were overgrown, there was no water in the pool, and the air-conditioners didn't work. We had ten servants and none of them worked either. If you wanted coffee, you had to go get it yourself. They acted like they worked, and the government acted like they worked, just like in Russia. They were paid in pesos, but the peso was worth nothing. "You've got this gorgeous property," I told Alarcón. "Why don't you do what they do in England? Sell someone the right to live there for thirty years and at the end of thirty years you get it back, and they've spent money to fix it up. They'd need lawn service and pool service and servants and they'd pay them and you'd employ people."

"God, that's a good idea," he said. They haven't done it yet.

The next day we went to the cigar store and bought forty boxes of Havana cigars, Montecristos, those big fat ones. Ricky had brought a big duffel bag and we filled it up. That night we went to have dinner with Castro and his chief of staff at one of the so-called palaces, a government building. We talked about shooting and doves and cattle, but when you talked to Castro, it was always more of a monologue on his part. You might ask, "What about the cattle business?" and thirty minutes later you ask, "What about shooting doves?" And thirty minutes later he's still talking. He talks, you listen, which was okay because he was knowledgeable.

As we were getting ready to leave, Ricky pulled out the duffel bag full of cigars. I was thinking, *What are you doing?*

He said, "President Castro, would you mind signing our boxes of cigars?"

Castro said, "I'd love to." He then proceeded to open every cigar box and sign each one. *Rick, Mucho gusto, Fidel. Tom, Mucho gusto, Fidel.* And on and on, personalizing every cigar box with the names Rick gave him.

We left Cuba and landed in Miami at around nine in the morning. The customs people took the tires off the plane, brought out the dogs, and they sniffed everything while we took our bags into immigration. The official asked us if we bought anything in Cuba.

"No sir, but we got gifts," Rick said.

He unzipped the duffel and there were forty boxes of Havana cigars inside.

"Gifts, huh?"

"Yes, go ahead and open them."

The official opened the boxes and saw that Castro had autographed every single one of them. The guy looked at Rick, who is a big guy, about six foot seven. Ted Turner, whom he later worked for at CNN, called him "the biggest Jew I've ever met."

"What do you do?" the official asked Rick.

"I'm a journalist," Rick said.

The guy then looked at me and asked, "And what do you do?"

"I'm with him," I said in a way that sounded like I'm the heat. The guy just zipped up the duffel and we left. He really thought I was the heat.

41

TENACITY
by Chris Sugrue

It was 1990, and I was an undergraduate at the University of Chicago majoring in economics and politics. I wanted a job so I could afford to take my girlfriend out. Through a friend of my sister and her husband, I was told to call a guy named Thomas H. Dittmer and ask for an interview, which I did. There was no Google back then, so I went to the library and used LexisNexis to look him up. The stories portrayed him as larger than life, and I was nervous as I got all dressed up and took the bus from campus to his office in downtown Chicago. When I finally got in to see him, the office was spectacular—Persian carpets, a suede couch, and a private conference room next door. He looked at me with his piercing blue eyes and he said, "Tell me everything about your life from the moment you were born, up until now, and how you got into my office."

While I was talking, he swiveled around in his chair to look at the computer screens and charts behind him. Then he started reading his mail and talking on the phone. I was talking to the back of his chair. I was only nineteen, so my life story wasn't that long. After about ten minutes, I was just sitting there and he was on the phone. A good twenty minutes later he turned his chair around and was shocked to see me. "What the fuck are you still doing here?" he said.

"I told you my life story like you asked me to do. Do you have any other questions?" I asked.

"Get the fuck out of my office," he said. I got up to leave and as I'm walking out the door, he says, "My door is open if you want to come back."

I left defeated, but the next day I got dressed up again, got on the bus, and went back to his office. His secretary was gone and Tom was about to leave for lunch. I poked my head in. "Do you have a minute?" I asked him.

"Who are you?" he asked.

"I'm the kid you threw out of your office yesterday and you told me to come back," I said.

He gave me a kind of a smile and said, "I didn't mean today." But I could tell there was a little melting of the facade. So, I went back every day for a week. Eventually he was telling people not to let me in. So each time I went back, I had to get through security, past the receptionist, and past his secretary. I had to linger and wait for doors to open and go in behind somebody, then wait until his secretary left her desk. Then when he'd see me, he'd say, "Get the fuck out of my office!" but I could tell he was enjoying it. "Don't you listen?" he would say. "What the fuck do you want from me?" I told him that I wanted to know how he made so much money. How did he become who he was? I really wanted to know. And he would throw me out again.

I drove him crazy.

Finally, Tom said that he would hire me if only to get me out of his office. They paid me $4.50 an hour, the minimum wage, to be a runner on the floor of the Exchange. I did everything I could to get close to him, and he did everything he could to keep me away. When I finished school I wanted to go back and work for Tom, but he told me that I should get other experience. I got a job working for the Catalyst Institute, a think tank in Chicago that did economic analysis and research and that Tom partly sponsored. They paid me $75,000 a year, which back then was a lot of money. I brought Tom my paycheck to prove it.

"Look at this," I told him. "This is where your money is going." He was horrified.

42

LITERALLY TAP DANCING

I had always wanted to tap dance, so for my fiftieth birthday I decided to learn how. I used to watch the June Taylor Dancers and Fred Astaire, and I would study everything they did, every move they made. I just loved those films. There was someone who worked in the office at Refco who had a parent who ran a dance school. I called the school.

"Tom Dittmer," I said.

"Yes?"

"I'd like to take some tap dancing lessons. I'll come down to the studio."

"No, no, no," she said.

"Why not?" I asked.

"Because I only teach little kids, and the first time you show up at my studio, a fifty-year-old dancing with my five-year-olds, their parents will take them away and I'll lose my business."

"You have a point," I said.

She told me she would come to my house and that I should get a tap floor, a mirror, and a barre. I had a three-car garage and I built three tap floors in it. The floors were hollow, which gave the taps good resonance. I hung a barre and plastic mirrors on the wall, and I practiced. The teacher—I wish I could remember her name!—would come out every Saturday and Sunday for about an hour and teach me the steps. She choreographed a routine for me, with a partner. I loved it! By the way, it's all about posture and balance, because you have to stand on one foot and tap the other one.

Then it was time to learn the routine to music.

"How do I do it with music?" I asked.

"Just listen to the music."

"Hell, no. I'm just trying to concentrate on what I'm doing."

After a lot of practice, I was able to tap and listen to the music and know when I was supposed to start and end and do the turns. I had to count the beats, but I couldn't move my lips because that was a no-no.

My plan was to tap at my birthday party, but my teacher told me that before that, I needed to have the experience of a public performance. The teacher had a friend who put on a talent show in Des Plaines for the blue-rinse set. Her friend would let us in the show Friday or Saturday night, but I had to buy out the whole show, which was $5,700. The money was to pay for the buses to pick up the old people and take them to the school auditorium. I was backstage, dressed in my tux, and I looked out into the audience and saw at least forty of my friends. Frannie had called them, and one of them even had a camera. I knew they were there just to make life rough for me. I was scared to death but I did it, about four minutes' worth. Then my friend with the camera went around and interviewed the old people in the audience.

"What did you think of Tom?" he asked one little woman.

"Oh, he had such a nice voice," she said.

"How did you like Tom's dancing?" he asked another person.

"Who? Was someone dancing?"

My friends were crying laughing.

A week before my birthday, I entered a talent show at the community center in Lake Forest. The next oldest performer was a five-year-old girl. I walked in and the mothers shielded their children. Who is this guy? Once again, I bought the whole house and I performed first, a half hour before the regular talent. There were about three hundred people in the audience that night, including the people from my birthday party. I performed my routine with my teacher. My friends booed a little and made fun of me, but when I finished, they threw flowers onto the stage. I had fun, but thank God there was no YouTube then.

I still have my tap shoes. Race cars didn't impress the girls when I was dating, but the tap shoes did.

43

NEW YORK AND CASTRO

Frannie was mad at me for leaving Lake Forest for New York. We had busy lives and lots of friends in Chicago. She sat on prestigious boards and committees, and she was a queen bee there. I was on the board of the Lyric Opera and was involved in all sorts of things, but my main priority was the business. Chicago had been the center of the universe from the '60s to the '80s, but I could see the game shifting from commodities to equities. When that big bull stock market started in '82, I knew New York was the place to be. I didn't go then because I didn't want to upset Frannie. But in 1994, we did move to New York into a brownstone we rented on 80th Street between Park and Lexington avenues. Sir James "Jimmy" Goldsmith, the British billionaire and tycoon, owned the house. Coincidentally, later on, Frannie would buy a house in Careyes, Mexico, and Jimmy would be her neighbor there. The townhouse was great; it had four stories and an atrium. Frannie's art collection and our Lake Forest furniture fit perfectly so we didn't have to go out and buy all new things.

In 1995, I started a hedge fund business with Edwin Cox, Jr. Ed was a Dallas businessman who had cattle holdings and energy ventures. His father, Edwin Cox, Sr., was a big oilman in Dallas, but I knew the Coxes through the cattle business. Back in '88, when Ed Jr. was on the board of InterFirst Bank in Dallas, he borrowed money from the bank. And though he repaid it, the trouble was he had signed over an oil trust as collateral. The trust was in both his and his father's names but his father had refused to sign it. Well, Ed Jr. signed it anyway, so he had given them collateral that he didn't have the right to give. The Justice Department wanted to make an example of him and gave him six months in prison and fined him $250,000.

I visited Ed Jr. when he was in prison, and after he served his time, I picked him up and took him home. Just before he left office in '93, George H. W. Bush pardoned Ed Jr., thanks to a call from Texas Governor Bill Clements. After the pardon, Edwin Sr. gave a big donation to the Bush library.

When I moved to New York in 1994, Ed moved too, and we started the hedge fund together. I was trading at Chase Bank, and David Puth, my guy there at the time, said, "You're our second biggest customer." I asked him who the first was. "Julian Robertson from Tiger Management, with a twenty-billion-dollar hedge fund." Julian started Tiger in 1980, and at his peak he was the biggest guy in the world of hedge funds. One of the best trades in those days was the dollar/yen. I'd trade billions in a day and could do it because I had leverage. I'd buy the dollar at 5 percent and sell the yen at a ½ percent, and the 4 percent "carry" was profit. The yen was also going down in value at the time, so it was a double bonus. That hedge fund business was fun and I did very well. Julian did even better.

★★★

In October of 1995, the world's leaders were coming to New York City to mark the fiftieth anniversary of the United Nations. Mayor Rudy Giuliani was having a big party on Saturday night at the World Financial Center to kick off the event, which was going to be the largest gathering of world leaders in history. Along with all the dignitaries and their entourages, there were some 3,000 agents from the FBI and the Secret Service. Manhattan was a mess of gridlock and street closures.

Both Yasser Arafat and Fidel Castro were coming to the UN event, but Mayor Giuliani didn't want either of them at his party. Arafat chose to go instead to a fund-raiser in his honor across the street from Giuliani's party, and I hosted a party for Castro.

Cuba did huge business with us and had hosted me several times there, so when the Cuban Consul General called to ask if I would entertain Castro, I said yes. I was returning the favor. Another reason I said yes was because I had at least a hundred brokers from literally every country in South America, and they really wanted to meet Castro.

To become a broker in those countries, you had to come from a good family. You're not a posthole digger's son. If you're the banker's son, you can open an office and get business. What was amazing was that all these brokers were dying to meet Castro, even the ones born in the United States. There were some brokers whose parents had fled Cuba, some of them having buried their silver and family treasures in their yards to keep them out of Castro's hands. Some of them wanted to go back and see if their valuables were still there.

So Castro, in a suit and tie, showed up at our house in New York for his party. We had ten tables of ten for dinner. He gave a little speech and met all the brokers. After dinner everyone went onto the terrace for Armagnac and Havana cigars. Castro had stopped smoking by then, but he was milling about, talking to everyone, and having a good time.

Little did I know that during the party the NYPD and Secret Service had towed away every car on the block. They didn't want any bombs going off and killing Castro. The house was a stone's throw from the Iraqi Consul, and we normally had the Iraqi Secret Service, the CIA, and the NYPD around there anyway. You could have left your door wide open and been perfectly safe. When the neighbors asked me what happened to their cars, I blamed the Iraqis.

44

GO MAKE ME MONEY
by Chris Sugrue

Look, I really want to come back and work for you," I told Tom.

"Well," he said, "I don't think you're stupid or worthless anymore, so you've gotten over those two barriers." Then he said he'd hire me.

"Great. What will I get paid?" I asked him.

"You can pick your salary, but it's under the condition that whatever you take from the company, you have to return two and a half times that amount every year," he said. "If you don't, you're fired. So choose carefully."

I went home and talked to my girlfriend, who is now my wife, and we chose $40,000, which was half of what I was getting paid at the time. I figured I could make $100,000.

"Fine," Tom said. "There are two rules: one, never lie to me. If you get into a situation that is out of your control, you come to me quickly. And two, never let a problem grow. When a problem gets out of control, it becomes a headache. Those are the conditions of your employment."

Then I asked him what to do. He said, "Go make me money."

At the time, Tom owned 51 percent of Refco and Phil Bennett and Tone Grant each owned 24.5 percent. Among the three of them there were factions within the company. If you supported one, the others hated you. I was in the Dittmer Camp and that was the strong camp, the majority camp. The guys in the other camps were always snapping at Tom's heels.

I was a young man and my father had left us when I was twelve. I needed counsel on big life decisions, like whom to marry, and I relied on Tom for help with those. When we were out one night, I told him that my girlfriend was mad because we had been dating for eight years and we were not engaged, and I didn't know what to do.

"If you want your kids to be like her," Tom told me, "then marry her because she will be the biggest influence in your kids' lives. If she's what you want for your kids, then don't waste any time."

We got engaged.

I had just started working for Tom again, I was twenty-five, it was 1995, and Refco gave me a big Christmas bonus. I didn't think I had earned it. Tom's generosity is significant. I went to the bank and told them I wanted the check in cash. I had never seen so much money in my life.

Tom and Frannie were going out to Borsheims Fine Jewelry in Omaha to go Christmas shopping for Frannie. Tom told me to come along with them to buy my engagement ring. I put all my cash in my briefcase and went to the airport and boarded Tom's Falcon.

They had opened the jewelry store on a Sunday morning especially for Tom. When we got there Frannie went off to what she called the "big ice" section, and I went to look at engagement rings. The salesperson pulled out the perfect diamond and I asked her how much it was. The price was the exact amount of my bonus check. I was thrilled and gave her the cash. Frannie told me I did a good thing because my wife would always be happy and proud of the ring.

Years later it occurred to me what a coincidence it was that the ring cost exactly what my bonus check was. Tom and I were out one night and I asked him about it.

"What do you think?" he asked me.

"That it wasn't a coincidence," I said.

"Of course it wasn't," he said. He knew the amount of my check and told Borsheims what to charge me, and he paid the difference. He never said anything about it for all those years. This is typical Tom.

At Refco, I reported directly to Tom. I settled into the hedge fund investments and learned other businesses as well. Every year it was the same: How much did you spend and how much did you take? Not only salary, but if you sent a FedEx, you paid for it. If you made a phone call, you paid for it. You paid for everything. Eventually I got better at managing the business, and we grew it, and he was very happy. All I wanted to do was hang out with him. I wanted to be his star. I would do anything to make him as much money as I could.

I went to him one day and asked him if he would sell the company if I could find a buyer. He said, "Yeah, sure, sure, go ahead." He wasn't really paying attention since I was a kid in my twenties and it was a silly thing for me to ask. Nevertheless, since I had access to the chairman of Refco, I had a certain amount of credibility with people. I went uptown to Lazard Frères and hired them to help me sell the company. Before the big Internet companies came to life, we thought electronic trading was the future and that AT&T would be the best partner. It was a big company, they connected people all over the world. So, I went with Lazard to pitch the chairman of AT&T, Bob Allen, to buy Refco. I was working like a devil to get this thing going and I was telling Tom that I really thought they were interested. I asked Bob Allen for $100 million for Tom's stake in the business and we would grow it from there. Lazard was doing all the back work to push it through. I got Tom to Midtown to meet with Michel David-Weill, then chairman of Lazard. He was an elegant Frenchman and an important international figure. Tom and Michel hit it off right away, and Michel said he liked the deal.

Tom still wasn't taking this or me seriously, but then it started to get serious. "I need you with me in Basking Ridge, New Jersey," I told him, "and we're going to meet with the chairman of AT&T."

He wouldn't go. "Bring Tone," he told me. "He is better at this stuff than I am." The problem was neither Tone nor Phil had any idea what was going on. "I'll talk to Tone. It'll be fine," he told me.

I'm thinking *I'm fucked*. But I'm also thinking if Tom calls Tone then maybe Tone won't hate me so much, and maybe the partners will think it's a good thing. Tone took the Falcon 900 out of Chicago to New Jersey, and I, along with several bankers, met him a half hour before the meeting. I hadn't talked to him at all before this, and I briefly told him what we were doing. He just nodded and listened. Then we went into this huge boardroom and made our pitch to Chairman Bob Allen, John Petrillo, the AT&T Chief of Strategy, and a host of others. Tone still wasn't saying a word. He just sat there.

"I like it," Petrillo said. "I think it would fit with our strategy." I couldn't believe it! I was just a twenty-six-year old kid and this was a big deal.

Tone gets up and says, "We don't want to do this," and he walks out of the room.

You can imagine the shock. They're thinking I'm crazy. "I have no idea what just happened," I tell the group in the room. I go back to New York and see Tom.

"Look, we had a deal on the table with these guys and Tone just shot it down and left."

Tom said, "That's tough luck, kid."

Fortunately other deals I worked on for Tom went better, including one with DG Bank that brought in $100 million. But Phil Bennett was always on my case, and my relationship with Tone wasn't good either. When Tom left the company, I no longer had an advocate. Phil sat me down and told me it was time for me to go.

"You've been okay here and you made us some money, but you should find something else to do," he said. So I did.

45

EVERYTHING CHANGED
BUT THE LOVE

In October 1996, Frannie and I celebrated our thirtieth wedding anniversary. We chartered the *Sea Goddess*—today it's changed hands and is called the *Sea Dream*—and took fifty couples, our friends, on a cruise. We divided people up into teams and performed skits and did all sorts of fun things on the ship. Every night was a party with a different theme, again all planned by Bruce Southworth. In Turkey we had a toga party at the amphitheater in Ephesus. When we walked up to the amphitheater, guys dressed in togas and gladiator sandals met us with trays of drinks and champagne. We kept walking and could hear the thumping of music by Michael Carney and his band, who had flown in for the evening, in the distance. By the time we reached the amphitheater, our guests were so excited they could hardly stand it.

We sailed on to Venice and rented villas where we picked up another hundred couples and had another party. We hired Diana Ross to entertain us at that one. She was so sweet and she was having such a good time that she wanted to keep singing all night. It was a hell of a party.

Then just a few months later, after thirty years of marriage, Frannie and I separated. We'd had several years when the marriage wasn't working and both of us were unhappy. We were mad at each other about the move to New York and mad at each other for being mad at each other. Frannie was unhappy in New York. And when Frannie was unhappy, I was unhappy.

In March of 1997, I called Frannie from the office and asked her to meet me at home. When we got home I said, "Honey, I want to talk to you. I've been thinking about getting a divorce for a while now."

She looked at me and said, "God, me too!" I asked her why she hadn't said anything before now. "I was scared," she said.

I was fifty-five years old. "You could have told me when I was fifty," I said. Of course I might have killed myself then—that wild life I was about to lead could have proven lethal. We nodded and stared at each other for a bit. In thirty years there had never been anyone else but Frannie. I never, ever cheated on my wife. I don't do that. That's not who I am.

Frannie and I went to lunch and talked about it, and about a month later I moved into a one-bedroom apartment in the Mark Hotel on East 77th street. We'd made our decision. I told her that I didn't see any reason to divorce because I didn't have anybody I was interested in dating, and if I did, I would tell her. She told me that she wasn't going to get married again. Once was enough for her, and marriage was an unsatisfactory relationship. Maybe it was just me she didn't like.

We had just bought a big house in Greenwich, Connecticut, on fifty-five acres with two lakes. David Easton did it all up and it was a showcase property. I bought it to try to keep Frannie happy, but I never spent a night there and she sold it when it was almost finished.

Fortunately, we didn't have the money problems many people have when they separate. We agreed on everything, got the money straightened out, and filed for a legal separation. I spent $5,000 on legal fees and she spent $3,000. We told our kids on May 26th. Alexis was graduating that June from Dartmouth and Jason was in Wyoming working as a National Outdoor Leadership School instructor. Then Frannie sent out a letter to our friends saying, "Tom and I are getting separated and we might get divorced. There's no reason to pick sides. We love all of you and each other and we hope we can all remain friends." We both signed the letter.

Even though it was what we both wanted, it was traumatic. I wanted someone to talk to about it and asked around for recommendations for therapists. I ended up seeing psychiatrist Nathan Schwartz-Salant twice a week for about six months. He told me I was afraid of standing up to women because of my strong mother, and he was probably right.

46

FROZEN PEAS
by Jason Dittmer

My mom and dad laughed and loved life together. They had challenges in their relationship, but they were a great team and great friends. One of the times I was most proud of my dad was when he and my mother decided to get divorced. Here they were in their fifties. My dad had built a wonderful life for his family, he had Refco, he had everything. I remember asking my dad how they were going to take thirty-plus years of life together and cut that up.

"We're not," he said. "Your mom has been my wife and she is the mother of my children. She gets everything." They were not going to have the animosity of having to split things up and that meant that we could continue to be a family, and that's what happened. The divorce didn't have a huge impact on me because I saw two people moving into another phase, connected, but not together.

We still spent holidays as a family. One Christmas, when we were at my mom's in Aspen, my father was recuperating from a face lift. The altitude made his face even more swollen than it already was, so we bought a bag of frozen peas to pack on his face, and he fell asleep on the sofa. A couple of hours later he woke and came walking into the kitchen. The "Birds Eye" print from the bag had transferred onto his face. We laughed at him, and he told us to go fuck ourselves. It was so funny. If anything ever went sideways, we always came together as a family, and Mom and Dad were always there for each other, no matter what.

47

THE F-WORD MAN
by Shari Ardhaldjian

Tom was still CEO of Refco when he started the MLC hedge fund company in New York with Ed Cox and Ralph Crocker. Ralph's wife was my connection to getting an interview with Tom for the position of executive assistant. We spoke for an hour and a half about everything from politics to the Armenian genocide. I thought maybe he just wanted to talk. The next day I was offered the job and was pleasantly surprised because I thought this was a guy who was going to make coming to work interesting. That was an understatement. He's the craziest person I've ever worked for.

Tom, Ed, and Ralph were all crazy guys and all different. Ed was this very Southern guy from Texas; Ralph Crocker was a Long Island guy; and then there was Tom from the Midwest, who was very, well, Tom-ish. The group was loyal, hard-working, and family-like, which was exactly what Tom was about.

Some of the folks on the Refco side of the business called Tom a cowboy because he was brash and brazen. He did what he thought would be

fun and good for business. That didn't always go so well with the accountants and the rule-makers, though. He came close to the line, but he
didn't cross it. He didn't break the law. It drove him crazy when customers took big risks, lost, and then wanted to sue him for it. You don't go
to Vegas and sue someone because you don't win at the slots.

For a short time, my in-laws were living with us in New York, and
we had one of those old answering machines. I came home one day
and my mother-in-law was beside herself.

"What's going on?" I asked her.

"I don't know, Shari, there's someone . . . I think you need to call
the police. A man left a message, he was swearing, he was looking for
you. He was a crazy man. Don't listen to it, it's so awful," she said.

I listened to the message.

"Shari, where's my fucking car?! I can't find my fucking car!!" He
basically said the F-word more than he said anything else. My mother-
in-law wasn't sure there was even a message in there.

"No. It's okay," I told her. "That's Mr. Dittmer. You know Mr.
Dittmer." She couldn't believe it.

My mother-in-law adored Tom. I had to tell Tom not to leave those
kinds of messages on my answering machine again.

I was always on him about his swearing. Tom likes to tell the story
about how one day I was on the phone chewing someone out and
using Tom's language. When I got off the phone I went into his office
and he was grinning at me.

"Okay," I said, "you corrupted me a little bit."

Now my husband tells me I cuss too much.

I got pregnant around the time Tom was selling Refco, and my husband and I decided to move to Boston. I continued working for Tom,
and he was fine with me working from home.

When my son was born, we named him Ardavasd, a very Armenian
name. Tom called the hospital every day to see how I was doing, and

when he heard our son's name, he said, "With a name like that he's never gonna get any fucking girls." That's a story we still tell in our family with great affection.

It has been seventeen years since I worked for him and we still stay in touch. He is one of the most amazing people I've ever met.

48

SEARCHING

People were fixing me up with dates all the time. Hey, when you own a Falcon 900 and they think you're rich, everyone has someone for you to date—but it doesn't make you special. I went out a few times in New York, but I kept it to neighborhoods away from the Upper East Side, so I could avoid running into Frannie and our friends. I also rented a house in the Malibu Colony and dated in Los Angeles. It was far enough away from Chicago and New York not to offend Frannie. For the first time in my life I was sowing my wild oats—a little late, but . . . I had hundreds of dates in a year and a half. I quit working and dated, and all my secretary did was arrange my dating schedule, make reservations, and send flowers and thank-you notes. I was searching for someone because I like being married. That's just how I am.

In August of 1998 I was invited to Martha Stewart's birthday party in Seal Harbor, Maine. Her house, *Skylands*, was built in 1925 for Edsel Ford, Henry's son, and it's beautiful. This was where I met Sandy

Hill Pittman. I didn't really know anything about her. I left the party with Charles Simonyi, Martha's beau at the time. Simonyi was the head of Microsoft's application software group—smart guy, but a little strange. He offered me a ride back to New York with him on his Falcon 50. When I got on the plane, Sandy was there. I thought she was a nice girl. I went my way and she went hers.

When Sandy was getting a divorce from Robert Pittman, she moved into my friend Sam Waksal's house in New York. I'd met Sam through Martha when he was dating Martha's daughter, Alexis. I went to visit Sam, and there was Sandy. Sam told me all about her and that she had been staying at his house for the past month while her new house was being renovated. I said hello to Sandy and went back to California. Then I would occasionally go back to visit Sam, and Sandy would be there. The friendship kind of evolved.

I was dating and going crazy with women everywhere, until one day I looked in the mirror and thought, *If my mother were alive, she wouldn't speak to me. I don't even like myself* anymore. It was over. So I got out of the rental house in Malibu, went back to New York, and rented an apartment in the Museum Towers, across the street from the Museum of Modern Art on East 53rd street.

Later that same year, I called Sandy and asked her to dinner. She was smart and good looking and she'd done interesting things like climbing the seven summits, the highest mountains on each of the seven continents. At the time the only downside I could see was that she wasn't particularly funny. After we'd been out a few times I read the book *Into Thin Air* by Jon Krakauer about the infamous 1996 Mount Everest expedition in which eight people died. Sandy was on the expedition. Some, including Krakauer, held her partially to blame. Krakauer made her out to be a spoiled, publicity-hungry bitch, but of course she had her own side of the story.

I should have known better from the very first date. I was driving a six-year-old 7-Series BMW. I pulled up in front of Sandy's new house and double-parked. I knocked on the door and she came out, grabbed the backdoor handle, and jumped into the back seat. Okay. I got behind the wheel and drove off. I stopped at a red light; she stepped out and got into in the front seat.

"So how poor are you?" she asked me.

"Pretty poor," I told her.

I was tired and disgusted with myself with all the running around I'd been doing, so Sandy and I started dating steadily. My lease was going to be up at the end of the year.

"Move in with me," Sandy said.

"No," I said. "I'm moving to London in January and I'm going to go to school. I need to be by myself and that's what I'm going to do."

"Then I'll go with you," she said.

Except I hadn't invited her. I don't know why I didn't stand up to her, but that has been a pattern in my life. Like my shrink had said, maybe it was because of my mother. I really wanted to go by myself and I knew exactly what I was going to do. I was going to trade a little, help a guy with a hedge fund, live in an apartment, and audit classes at the London School of Economics. I had it all worked out.

I gave up my apartment, Sandy kept her house in New York, and we moved to London together. I rented a house and we spent a year there. I never went to school because all we did was work out, go to lunches and dinners, and play around.

One night at Massimo's Restaurant in London, I proposed. A week earlier we had seen Alexis in France, and I called her with the news. "You'd better tell Mom," Alexis said.

I called Frannie. "I'm getting married," I said. "You need to file the divorce papers."

"I thought once was enough," she said.

"Not for me," I said. "I thought our first twenty-five years were great, honey." She hung up on me. I called her back the next day to apologize. I told her our marriage was great. It just didn't wind up the way it should have, but it was wonderful and it didn't turn me off from getting married.

"It did me," she said.

49

THE END OF AN ERA

At Refco we bought three-year Government T-Bills every month with customer funds. When the note rolled off, we took whatever money there was in interest—4 or 5 percent—to keep as our profit and bought more three-year notes. We never varied. We only bought three-years and that was it. No speculation, no risk, no downside. In 1999 interest rates went down, so the notes we had bought earlier at higher rates would make us a fortune. I remember telling Phil Bennett that. "I got out of all of them about two months ago," he said. This made me wild. I couldn't believe it. We'd been doing this three-year deal for thirty years, and it worked perfectly, and he just decided to end it and not even discuss it with me?

I went home that night and I was mad at Phil but madder at myself. This was someone I had trusted completely and had given more and more control to. For him not to have even discussed with me something we had been doing for thirty years . . . well, I figured it was time for me to leave. What else didn't I know about? What else had he changed? What else had he done?

Turned out he'd done a lot. Another disastrous deal I didn't learn about until we were dividing up the company had happened a dozen or so years earlier. On October 19, 1987, Black Monday, the stock market broke 37 percent in one day. A trading customer of ours lost $150-some-million dollars on a single trade. Phil let him off the hook, meaning we, Refco, had to absorb the loss. Phil's aim was to keep Refco from being sued and to keep it out of the papers because it would have looked bad for the company, even though we'd done nothing wrong. The customer, Victor Niederhoffer, was a pro speculator who had been trading for years. He had a PhD in mathematics from the University of Chicago and was George Soros's partner. Not exactly a neophyte. The Refco guys taking his orders weren't there to give advice and weren't supposed to. But this was such a monumentally bad, crazy-high-risk S&P options trade, no one should have taken it. Refco's commission was $150,000, and it cost us a $150 million.

Where was I? Downstairs trading the hedge fund and having fun and making money.

Of course they came to me and told me about it, but what I didn't know is that we never collected any of what Niederhoffer owed us. It wasn't until twelve years later when we were dividing up the company that I found out. Why not? I asked. I thought we could have gotten at least some of the money back. Niederhoffer had money, he had houses and real estate. That's when I learned that Phil had gone to Victor to get a release from him saying he didn't have to pay us back, and that he wouldn't sue, and therefore Refco would avoid bad publicity. Though I'd had misgivings about selling the company, this Niederhoffer bombshell confirmed my worst fears.

My biggest argument against selling had been losing my leverage. Leverage was the power I had with Refco, and it was huge. I could buy $80 million worth of stock and put up no money. I could buy Brazilian CDs that were paying 20 percent with no money down. The same thing with the dollar/yen. You're short yen and long dollars. The interest rate on the yen is a ½ percent and the dollar is 5 percent, so on every billion dollars you made $50 million a year. You're getting 5 percent interest and you're only paying out a ½ percent. With the leverage I had, I could trade billions of it for no money. So walking away from that kind of leverage was a big deal for me. I thought I might never have that kind of power again, and I was right, unfortunately.

Pop and I had built that company from the ground up thirty years before, almost to the day. It was a lifetime. When we first started it was like the Wild West. We were gunslingers and all the cowboys worked for us, and people couldn't believe some of the shit we did. We were brash and brave and we did things no one else had ever done, and we made money at it. It was fun. When I had the hedge fund with Edwin Cox in New York, I used the leverage I had with Refco, and it was hugely profitable and fun. Fun was making money. But, like any business, the more it matured, the more lawyers and accountants got involved, and they aren't so much fun. Refco at the end was different from Refco at the beginning, by a lot.

Once I made the decision to sell the company, the papers were drawn up within one or two days and Refco was sold to Phil Bennett and Tone Grant. Right after that I cashed out on the feedlots and ranches, too. Once I left Refco, I had a feeling those days of fun were gone.

50

MOVING TO CALIFORNIA

Sandy and I spent New Year's 1999 in Cabo San Lucas, Mexico. Then we flew to California and rented a car to drive from San Francisco to Los Angeles. Back in the late '60s, Frannie and I had driven the same route, and when we got to the Santa Ynez Valley, I told Frannie that someday I was going to have a ranch and maybe retire there. It was the prettiest ranch country I'd ever seen. I told Sandy how I'd always thought of having a ranch in Santa Ynez, so we got a real estate broker and looked at fifty or so ranches.

When we got to Rancho La Zaca, which belonged at the time to the actor James Garner and his wife, it was foggy and rainy but you could still see the Santa Ynez Mountains. The land and vistas were spectacular. We married in 2001, we got along okay, and one of the best parts was that we really explored California. I'd read a lot of books about California and we drove up to the Pacific Northwest, visiting the national parks on the way. It's a hell of a state.

By now, Frannie was living full time in Aspen and had become active in the community. We had been going to Aspen since the '70s and had many close friends there. Our children grew up there. Hell, we all grew up there. Frannie and I remained close and often spent holidays together there with the kids.

Now, with Sandy in the picture, there was a problem: Frannie and Sandy did not like each other. I guess Sandy felt threatened by my relationship with Frannie. When Sandy wanted to go to Aspen for Christmas and New Year's, I would go along with it because that's what Sandy wanted, and because I wanted to see Frannie and the kids, so we'd rent a house there. But the kids wouldn't come over and obviously neither would Frannie. I think Sandy wanted to go there just to poke at Frannie. Frannie asked me, "Why, with all the ski resorts in the world, do you want to come to Aspen?"

I was such a pussy.

51

REFCO SELF-DESTRUCTS

Phil Bennett and Tone Grant sold 57 percent of Refco to Thomas H. Lee & Partners in 2004 for $583 million in stock. I got paid my $120 million and then Refco went public. They sold 26.5 million shares to the public at $22, and by the end of the day the company was valued at $3.5 billion. It was a ride for them, not me. I was out of it.

In October of 2005, just months after the IPO, word came out that Phil had been hiding $430 million in debt since 2002. He paid it back, but that didn't keep him from being charged with securities fraud. On October 12, he was arrested. When everything blew up, I bought Refco stock at $5. It wasn't too many days earlier that it was trading at $50, and I thought it was a steal. I bought it and lost about $300,000. What should have happened was that Bank of America should have bought it for nothing, but that's not what happened. On October 17, 2005, Refco filed for Chapter 11. The stock dropped to eighty cents a share.

To think that only the Chicago Mercantile cleared more trades than Refco. Refco was second—in the world—and bigger than the

Chicago Board of Trade itself. Eventually the Merc and CBOT merged, but imagine if some big bank or other had bought Refco and transformed it into an exchange. Refco might have become *the* commodities exchange. That's all speculation, of course, but it's conceivable.

When Refco went down, the government wanted my $120 million back, and I was absolutely shocked. That $120 million was part of my deal when I sold Refco to Phil and Tone in 1999. Part of the deal was that I could not be anywhere near Chicago or New York, because Phil and Tone were afraid I might undermine their authority. I couldn't even go to the office. That's how I got out to California. At the time, I had a penthouse in New York on 61st and Park, 5,000 square feet with a big terrace and its own elevator. I sold it, but I wish I had it now.

I talked to my lawyer, Marshall Eisenberg. I had been gone more than six years. What about the statute of limitations? I thought anything over a year and a half was out. Marshall said, "This is a high-profile case and they want to beat up on everybody. They can do anything they want." I asked him what my odds were of fighting it. "Odds of fighting?" He said. "What are you talking about? You've already done this once, and what did it cost you?"

"Ten years of my life and $17 million," I said.

"Well, now, you're a little bit older. Do you want to do this for another ten or twenty years?" Marshall said.

"I haven't been to the office in more than six years. I haven't even talked to Phil since 1999. How can I be liable for any of this?"

"Because they're going to say you are," said Marshall.

So I didn't fight them. They make the rules. The government has infinite money and infinite time. I figured I would probably die in the process, so just give it back.

Both Phil and Tone were convicted of various fraud charges. Phil got sixteen years in prison. He wanted to go back to England to serve his time because his family was there, but they wouldn't let him. After he serves his sentence, he'll be deported back there anyway. He paid back the $430 million, but they still put him in prison. Tone got ten years in a minimum-security prison in Minnesota and died there in 2015. Once it went down, Marshall said I couldn't talk to Tone or Phil. That's too bad because I would have gone to see them.

52

THE VIRGIN ISLANDS

Sandy and I lived between New York and California, and then we lived in the US Virgin Islands. There was a tax law that said if you bought real estate in the USVI, lived there so many months a year, and employed at least twelve people, you could file your return there and pay 3 percent federal tax. The law was made for Hess Oil and is still there. Puerto Rico is the same way. So around 2001, we decided to go live in St. John. We did that for three years.

There were two schools in St. John, one located downtown in a warehouse, and one on the hill. Both were floundering. In 2004, I bought the land adjacent to the school on the hill so they could build soccer fields, basketball courts, and enough schoolrooms to accommodate students from kindergarten through high school. We got out of the lease in the warehouse and combined the two schools to become Gifft Hill School. I brought in two teachers in from Providence St. Mel, and Paul Adams and Jeanette Butala would come down a couple of times a year to advise and consult. In 2004, the first senior class in

St. John's history graduated. The Gifft Hill School was featured in the PBS series *Visionaries* in 2016. I am very proud of that school.

As a reward, the IRS decided to rake me over the coals. They said I couldn't do what I was doing with federal taxes. I argued that this wasn't some fancy accountant's trick; it was law. The IRS basically said that they didn't give a shit, and as a result I spent somewhere in the neighborhood of $700,000 in lawyers' fees and another ten years of my life fighting them.

I won, but the thing is, when the government comes after you like that, they don't have to prove you're wrong. They accuse you, and *you* have to prove you're innocent. I was lucky that I could afford to do that, but most people can't, and it's not like they reimburse you for your legal fees. Besides, if and when you win, you can never get the time back. The only winners are the lawyers.

53

ALONE AGAIN

Sandy and I were doing okay. It was expensive being married to her, but okay. She was so organized that even now in my phone are contacts for every best restaurant in the world, every best hotel, bakery, everything. I probably have 6,000 contacts because she detailed and cross-referenced everything—leather goods, Hermès, Paris, jewelry, kids' names, birthdays. If you want somebody to fix a priceless vase, she had it in the phone.

Jason wouldn't spend time with Sandy, but Sandy and Alexis got along fine. Alexis and Sandy would do things like go surfing in the morning, have the plane pick them up in Santa Barbara, then go to Mammoth to ski in the afternoon, then fly back home by dinner.

The problem was that when Sandy told a story, there was always a spin. I noticed it, but I ignored it for a long time. One night in New York I came home and she said, "We have to go out with the Lebenthals tonight."

"Who?"

"The Lebenthals. Oh, they're worth billions," she said.

"Well, they're not going to give us any money, so why do we care?"

"They're wonderful, you'll love them. They've invited us to dinner," she said.

"We've been out five nights in a row, do we have to go out again?"

"Yes!"

We met this nice young couple at Le Cirque in the Bloomberg Building. She was the Lebenthal, and he was married to her. I was talking to him about their family business, and then I asked how they knew Sandy. He told me Sandy called them to have dinner, and that they didn't know her before. That was the clearest sign for me that she just wasn't trustworthy. If you lie about something like that, and it's not even important, what does that tell you? From that moment on, I started to question everything Sandy had ever told me. When we got home, I asked how she knew the couple.

"Well, you know," she said. "Friends for a long time." Sandy was creative with the truth and there was no gray area in her stories. I always wondered about that.

What I didn't know at the time was that she always had a game plan for our marriage.

Around 2007, Sandy asked for a postnuptial agreement. I'd been facing two major lawsuits—the Refco clawback and the St. John residency tax deal. I stood to lose everything, and Sandy was scared. She wanted $10 million in cash now, and $1 million for every year we were married. She also wanted to keep the $10 million insurance policy on my life, and to keep the ranch. I wasn't about to sign any postnup. "Don't they call that extortion?" I said to her. She didn't think that was very funny.

Two years earlier I'd gone to talk to my lawyer, Marshall, about divorcing her, but I didn't go through with it. At sixty-six I was too old to do the whole dating thing again, and I didn't want to sit at the ranch in the middle of nowhere by myself. So I changed my mind.

"You're making a big mistake," Marshall said.

"Maybe so," I said.

In May of 2008, Sandy and I were at the ranch, sitting outside at the big round table where we had most of our meals. It was a Sunday, and we'd hosted a "salon" for the journalist Christopher Hitchens and had a bunch of people come for lunch and to hear him speak. After everyone had left, Sandy and I were talking about the day. Suddenly someone tapped me on the shoulder. I turned around and there was a man I'd never seen before in my life.

"Are you Tom Dittmer?" he asked me. And then he served me with divorce papers in my own house!

Sandy started crying. "Oh, I love you so much, I love you so much, but I have to protect myself."

Protect herself from what? From me being poor?!

After I was served the papers, I got in my car to go get an ice cream and I called Frannie to tell her the news.

"Jesus Christ, it's about time," Frannie said. "But you're such a chicken shit! You should have filed years ago, you dumb sonofabitch!"

Ten minutes after I hung up with Frannie my phone started lighting up. People were calling to say they wanted to see me, to ask me if I wanted to go hunting, if I wanted to come visit. All my old friends who didn't want to be around Sandy were back in play. Frannie had called them. I loved it.

But I was still being investigated, fighting lawsuits, and Refco had gone down in flames. It felt like my life was falling apart, and I was alone again.

54

A FAMILY AGAIN
by Alexis Dittmer

Sandy and I took to each other at first, and my mother was lovely about it. She didn't get in the way of my relationship with Sandy; she never said anything about it. Sandy and I were sporty. We liked to do things together—surf, hike, go on adventures, and she was a lot of fun. She showered me with attention, not like a mother figure, but more like an extravagant friend. I did realize, however, that my mother, my brother, and a lot of people in my parents' life didn't feel the same way about her that I did. I also knew that if she could get something from you, she would, and I imagine she viewed her relationship with me as the ultimate currency with my father.

I don't think Sandy and my father made a great couple. There was no balance. My father and mother had a dynamic, energized relationship. Dad and Sandy's was over the top and they brought out the worst in each other in certain ways. It was outrageous and not in a good way.

My relationship with Sandy fell apart while I was planning my wedding in 2006. I had the idea that a stepmother would dress nicely, show up, and act normal. She was incredibly creative, and when it came to throwing parties she was a force of nature. But with my wedding, I realized that for her it was less about my wishes and more about creating an event. That was the beginning of the end for us. We were still friendly, but my connection to her was broken at that point.

Not long after that, the wheels came off Dad and Sandy's relationship. After they separated, Dad came to Aspen. All of our friends came over and we had a ball. It was great. It was the beginning of the rest . . . of life now. Everyone was reconnecting. It was good for all of us.

55

CAROLINA ON MY MIND

Ironically, I would never have met my wife, Frances Schultz, if it hadn't been for Sandy filing for divorce and my having to leave the ranch. On June 1, 2008, I moved back to New York and into Frannie's apartment. I had a few fix-up dates, but my appetite wasn't the same. I was sixty-seven this time, not fifty-five, and I wasn't nearly as rich or as cute.

Parker Gentry is a good-looking gal and a friend whom we shot with up in Millbrook, New York. She's from North Carolina, is a hell of a shot, and she plays polo. "I've got a girl for you from North Carolina," she said on the phone.

"Great," I said.

Parker gave me the number and I called Frances, but it took a month for me to get on her dance card. Finally, we had our first date at La Goulue, and I arrived early. She walked in and she was tall and gorgeous. Perfect. I looked at her and thought, *There is a God.*

We talked and laughed for hours. She was charming, smart, accomplished, and really funny—and she had this great Southern drawl.

Afterwards I walked her home and we air-kissed. I took her out again, and air-kiss, air-kiss. I mean I took her out six times and all I was getting were air-kisses. I'm into thousands of dollars for dinners at this point. Not only that but we do the air-kiss two blocks from her apartment because, I suspect, she doesn't want her doorman to think she's a slut. But she told me that she had just broken an engagement and was a bit gun-shy about new relationships. On our sixth date, which, by the way, was going to be my last, she finally asked me if I'd like to come up for a drink. Gee, I think so! That was the first time we kissed. She's a good kisser.

There's a big gap between an Iowa farm boy and a Southern belle in the way you view life and look at things. It's a stretch for Frances, coming from the East Coast to California, and then being here at the ranch in the middle of nowhere, but she's taken to it well. Life is good. The first gift she ever gave me was a little red cowboy suit.

We were together for four years before we got married. Both of our families were there, including Frannie and my kids, the way it was supposed to be. They love Frances and she loves them right back.

56

WE GOT LUCKY
by Frances Schultz

When Tom and I first met I didn't know anything about him, though I did vaguely remember the name Refco. Given that I had recently and monumentally screwed up a relationship, I wasn't all that keen to enter another anytime soon. But the occasional date, okay. When Parker Gentry called and wanted to fix us up, I said sure. He sounded interesting.

When I walked into La Goulue, our then-favorite neighborhood canteen, on a Sunday night in October, there was a handsome, distinguished-looking man sitting alone at the back corner table. I knew it was Tom. He stood up when I came to the table—major points for manners—and literally within seconds I thought, *Yep, this could work*. Isn't that crazy? I sat down and he had this great laugh. He's a storyteller and I'm a storyteller. It was a great, fun night.

He was in New York that first year we were dating. He liked my friends, they liked him, and they all thought he was a good match for me. That he was not yet divorced put sort of a brake on our getting too serious in the beginning, and that was fine. His divorce was toxic, consuming, and Pyrrhic, and it went on for four years. Honestly, if I had to do it again I think I'd say, "call me when it's over." And then there were the lawsuits going on at the same time, which would have had devastating consequences if he lost, and of course the Refco claw-back he did lose. Those four years were tough for him and sometimes tough for us together.

One day he said to me on the phone, probably after a bad conversation with his lawyer, "What do you see in me, anyway? I'm old, I'm beat, I'm broke, and I'm not even divorced yet."

"Well," I said, "you're the only broke guy I know with a driver and a jet. But more importantly, you're taller and you weigh more." He roared with that laugh of his. And that was that. As for the fifteen-year age difference, I joked that he was older, but I had had cancer, so we were even. Plus, it's fun to tease him.

One day he asked me, "Do you know who was on the Wheaties box when I was a kid?"

"Ben Franklin?" I said.

After a year or so Tom moved back to the ranch, and I commuted from New York. I'm a writer and can do what I do from most any-where. I couldn't get over how beautiful it was there, and clearly he was in his element. Exactly how and when we decided to marry I don't recall, and eventually we decided to set a date even though Tom's divorce still wasn't final. Whether the actual wedding took place that day or not, we were going to celebrate.

We went through all the motions from planning the ceremony to sorting out the prenup. The legal bits were straightforward and easy, no drama. But then my lawyer called to caution me.

"What are you talking about?" I asked.

"Just don't go into business with him," he said.

"Whoa, whoa, whoa," I said. "I know the gossip around Tom, but if I've misjudged the character of my future husband, I need to know. So, please keep your clock running and get to the bottom of it. I want to put this to rest one way or the other."

A few weeks later the lawyer called me back, almost chuckling, to say that not only did he find the rumors to be untrue, but quite the opposite. Tom Dittmer, he said, was not only a pretty good guy, but a stand-up guy. I knew it, of course, but the journalist in me wanted to be able to say, definitively, "Yes, I had those rumors officially investigated, and they are not true, end of story."

The divorce was made final just ninety-one days before our wedding. Let's hear it for the bride and groom from AARP!

It's always heartwarming and flattering when your friends and family show up for you, but the biggest honor that day was that Frannie came. In the early days of Tom's and my relationship it was a bit of an adjustment for me to accept that Frannie was in the picture, but it soon became clear that she would also be my friend. We were one for all and all for one. I liked her and came to love her. It was impossible not to. I referred to her jokingly as my wife-in-law.

The Dittmer family was back together again, and I was lucky to be a part of that. I never had my own children, but I can't imagine better ones than Jason and Alexis. They are two of the most amazing, smart, funny, attractive, cool people I know. Jason's wife, Allison, and the grandchildren are wonderful too. I wish we saw them more. Now I sound like an old doting grandmother.

So here I am with my cowboy. One thing we will never do is bore each other. We are both big personalities with our own full plates. Our relationship is complex and sometimes challenging, but I've loved finding our rhythm together. Our backgrounds are different in some ways, and naturally that plays out in our respective views of the world and how we get along in it. I come from an old North Carolina family and a privileged upbringing. I've worked hard in my career as a writer, but I was fortunate that I did not have to struggle for the material things.

When we first began seeing each other, and after I'd done a little research on him, I found the courage to ask Tom if it was true about him trying to corner the cattle market. It sounded terribly scandalous to me at the time.

"No," he said, "I *did* corner the cattle market."

I burst out laughing but pressed on.

"So you always pushed the envelope. How come?" I asked him.

"I just wanted to get from point A to point B," he said. "And that's how I got there."

Lord knows we have different communication styles, to put it mildly. But what matters is that we share common values centered on family, character, integrity, and trust, and that is our core. We both grew up in small, rural communities, and we both benefited from that. We both grew up side by side with rich and poor. Family was everything to both of us, and we both had strong mothers who were tremendous influences in our lives. I laugh when I think about my mother and Tom together. She died three years before we met, but they would have been a hoot together. I don't know who would have out-flirted the other. She wouldn't have cared a thing about his pedigree, just that he was a good guy and he was good to me. And . . . she would have loved his dancing. I love his dancing, too.

He lets me be me. He supports me and cheers me on and makes me feel like a star. Not all wives get that, and not all wives have husbands who love and respect women as a whole, and he does. I am truly blessed, and we're having a ball.

57

GONE IN A MOMENT

On February 5, 2014, the single-engine plane flying Frannie from Puerto Vallarta, Mexico, to her house in Careyes went missing.

Jason called to tell me, but we didn't know any details, just that it had been off the radar for thirty minutes. It didn't look good, but we didn't give up hope. The people who run the airplanes down there are good at what they do, and my kids still use them. The pilot, Alberto Navarro, had logged 25,000 hours of flight time, which is as many as most commercial pilots have. He was so good that one time he lost the engine in a Pilatus, which is a single-engine propjet, and he managed to land it on a highway. The guy was a stud. This time he wasn't so lucky.

They found the wreckage the next morning. The plane went down so hard there wasn't much left. They reckon it hit the ground at two hundred miles per hour. It was just bad luck.

It was in this tragic moment that Frances really shined. She, the kids, Reverend Randall Day, and his husband, Billy Hurbaugh, took care of all of us and arranged the memorial services in Aspen and Chicago.

The kids are still healing. Losing your mother is hard, and you think about her every day.

The grandkids called her Fifi. Every time one of them does something cute, I think, *I wish Fifi could see it.* It goes on forever.

Losing Frannie was big. She was a great wife, mother, and grandmother. She had style, she was tall and beautiful, and she had that irresistible Texas drawl. She was never afraid to speak her mind and she had a big laugh that people always remembered. She had an eye and passion for art and was a major player in the art world. I'm still pissed at her for dying. Before she died, we'd talk at least four days a week. We'd bitch about the kids, and then she would bitch about me. Frannie and I had thirty years of marriage and two kids together. We had fun and I loved her. I miss her every single day.

58

F-1
by F-2

Everybody got a kick out of Frannie being F-1 and me being F-2, including Frannie and me. I was in my office at the ranch on that awful day when Tom came to tell me Frannie's plane was missing. When there was no word by late afternoon, we asked the children to come to us so we would all be together.

The next morning Tom and I were up before dawn, and Reverend Randall was at the house by ten. God bless him. Jason, Alexis, and Tom were on the phone constantly—to the Embassy, to the State Department, to the police, to the caretaker at the house in Careyes. Jason is fluent in Spanish, thank heaven. To have a logistical nightmare on top of this horrific tragedy was just surreal. Sweet Allison was seeing to their precious little boys, who at nine and seven were bewildered and subdued. The way the children and Tom handled it, and themselves, with such courage and grace, was remarkable.

If ever there was a time I was glad to be from a big Southern family and a small Southern town, it was then. Planning family gatherings and funerals is in my DNA. I just wanted to be there for them however I could, to honor their privacy and their grief, and to share in that but also to know my place. I hope I did.

As shocked as we all were by Frannie's death, I was also shocked by the depth of my own grief. *Damn,* I thought selfishly, *we were just getting going.*

59

MY MOTHER
by Alexis Dittmer

Frances and my father had been dating for a while before we met her. When she came into our lives, it was calm and not shocking or abrasive. She was easy to be around, not dramatic. Wow, that was different.

More and more I feel like she is this wonderful counterpoint to my father. She's lovely and he behaves around her. She just keeps him in check in a really nice way. She and my mother got along very well, and once Frances came along, our family got back to laughing and all being great friends. She was wonderful.

Like my brother says, my dad has been with some women who have made him not the best version of himself, and then he's been with my mom and Frances. Frances and Mom brought out the best in my dad.

My husband Chris and I had adopted a baby girl around Thanksgiving of 2013, when Mom and all of us were with Dad and Frances at the ranch. After three weeks, the birth mother had a change of heart and took the baby back, which was allowed by California law. It was devastating and I was in such a state of sadness that I didn't go to Mom's in Aspen for Christmas that year. And I never saw my mother again. She died in February. I was overcome with grief. Maybe losing the baby primed me to snap into action with my mother's death—like wow, I just went through this, I know how to do this and I know how to bounce back from it.

Then, in the summer of 2014, we secured a new birth mother and had a second baby on the way. Right after we heard that news, I found out that I was pregnant with twins, which, sadly, I miscarried. But our daughter Piper was born in Athens, Georgia, on August 2. She was premature and weighed three pounds, but she was strong and breathing on her own. Piper came to us at the perfect time. It seemed meant to be, and I felt like it was my mother's doing. I got the right little soul.

Six months before Mom died she had been thinking of leaving Aspen. I said, "Why don't you move back to Chicago?" She started looking for apartments the next day, found one, and put a deposit down. She was looking forward to growing old in a place she loved.

It was when my mother died that Frances really showed up in a major way. The obituary she wrote—oh my God, there was no way I could do it. Frances just said, "I've got this." It was beautifully written and funny and she completely captured our mother. Frances was so unbelievably helpful and so lovely.

60

MOM
by Jason Dittmer

Other than the loss of our grandparents, which was really hard for my dad to accept, Alexis and I had had a tragedy-free life, and that's pretty great. Our first real tragedy was my mom's death.

Nobody knows what happened. It was a good plane, a single-engine Mooney. My mom was probably in the copilot's seat because she had her pilot's license and loved sitting up front. Alberto had flown around the world in that plane and had made several emergency landings in it. If the plane was intact, he was going to be able to land it and live. Even if the pilot had been incapacitated, my mom could have flown the plane.

What little data they were able to collect showed that the plane went down in a nosedive. For that to have happened, there had to have been some kind of catastrophic structural failure. When Alexis and I flew down there we were in a little plane, and at 7,000 feet, I saw a massive turkey vulture sweep past us. My theory is a vulture or something came through the windshield or hit the tail. My mom and Alberto would have both been killed immediately.

Maybe my sister and I say this just to comfort ourselves, but my mom was 5'11" and strong as hell, and she was unafraid of almost everything except for getting old. She didn't like getting old. If you were going to write the final chapter in my mom's book, this isn't a terrible one to write. I miss her and I think about her every day, but this is a fitting final chapter. The only thing cooler would be if she staged her own death and is now running a rebel force down in Ecuador.

61

DESTINY
by Billy Hurbaugh

I grew up in Palm Beach, Florida, and New York City and went to school part of the year in each place. Three blocks south of us in Palm Beach was Tarpon Island, a legendary property situated in Lake Worth off of Everglades Island. It's stunning, with tennis courts, a helipad, swimming pool, and a beautiful house. I heard a man named Thomas Dittmer from Chicago had purchased it.

As a kid I liked to fish off the bridge to Tarpon Island. One day when I was about fourteen I was there fishing when a Rolls Royce sped up and screeched to a halt, nearly hitting me. A gray-haired gentleman rolled down the window.

"Who the fuck are you?" he said with a hint of a smile and a glint in his eye.

"My name is Billy," I said.

"What are you doing on my damn bridge?" he asked.

"I'm sorry. I'll get off it," I said. I got on my moped pretty damn fast and peddled home.

I didn't know anything about Mr. Dittmer but it turned out that his stepfather, Ray Friedman, and his wife, Maria, were good friends of my parents.

Thirty-five years later, my husband, Reverend Randall Day, was called to be the rector of St. Mark's Episcopal Church in Los Olivos, California, where we now live. One night Frances, then a new St. Mark's parishioner, invited us to dinner at Rancho La Zaca. When I met Tom I flashed back to being that fourteen-year-old boy on this man's bridge. He hadn't changed a bit.

"Oh, my goodness," I said. "You're Tom Dittmer from Palm Beach."

"What?!"

"I'm Billy Hurbaugh from Palm Beach, and you owned Tarpon Island."

"I did, I did."

I reminded him of the incident on the bridge and he claimed it never happened, but it did because I distinctly remember the car and that his ski instructor had given it to him. I never dreamed I would come across him thirty-five years later.

Tom and Frances have become two of our closest friends and we dine together almost weekly. One night we were all going to dinner and a movie, and I'd gone to the restaurant earlier in the day to pay for dinner, because it's impossible to pick up a check with Tom. Then I went to the movies and bought tickets and popcorn for the four of us. While I was doing this I told the guy at the movie theater, "I think my friend Tom Dittmer comes to the movies a lot with his dog."

"Oh, yeah," the guy said, "the gray-haired fellow. He comes at two o'clock when there's no one else here." If no one else shows up, they don't want to show the film, but Tom makes them show it anyway. Then he talks on his phone during the movie and makes them turn up the volume because he can't hear.

Tom doesn't attend church much, but he enjoys Randall's company and they discuss each week's sermon, and what's going on in the world and how Tom can help people, or where his help is most needed. He likes to hear Randall's opinion on things. We see a side of Tom that many people do not. Around town some people who knew him during his marriage to Sandy ask us, "What are you doing with him?" because they had such bad reputations. In truth you'll never find a more loyal, trusted friend than Tom.

There are six flagpoles at the entrance to the Dittmer ranch and they always fly the state flag of the people who are visiting. So we thought it would be funny, after having about a hundred dinners there, to give him a gay pride flag. He had no idea what it was when he unwrapped it but he was overjoyed that it was a flag.

"I love this!" he said. He then wrapped it around himself like a cape and said, "What is it?"

"It's the gay pride flag," we said.

"I love it even more!" he said, booming with that laugh of his.

The next time we visited the ranch, he had the rainbow flag flying. When we got to the front door we said to Frances, "We've got good news and bad news."

"What's the good news?" Frances asked.

"The good news is that we can assure you Tom is straight."

"And the bad news?"

"The gay pride flag is upside down on your flagpole."

When we got the news of Frannie's death, Tom and Frances asked us to lunch to discuss how they were going to proceed. They were both in shock, but they were in control and focused on what had to be done. As things progressed, they planned the two services for Aspen and Chicago, and Randall was heavily involved in that process with Frances.

In Aspen as we walked to Christ Church for the service, we passed the first house that Tom and Frannie had bought with Memrie and Perry Lewis, and Tom reminisced about the time Frannie decided to make popcorn and didn't know to put the lid on the pan. Ten years later they were still finding popcorn all over the place.

After the service, Frannie's reception at the Hotel Jerome was going full blast, with close to four hundred people despite a raging blizzard. All of a sudden, the electricity cut out. The room went pitch black. For a moment there was silence; then everyone said, "Frannie's at it now!" And then the lights flickered back on. It was very dramatic.

As we were leaving the next day for Chicago, Randall handed me the duffel bag containing the urn of Frannie's ashes. "Whatever you do," Randall told me, "don't lose sight of this." So I stood outside waiting because you never want to be late with Tom. Even if you're ten minutes early, you're fifteen minutes late. I was standing in the cold with our Bichon Frise, Ike, in one arm and Frannie's ashes in the other when a bellman asked if I was headed for the airport.

"Yes, sir," I answered.

He took the duffel and put it in a black SUV. With all the commotion—there were fourteen of us and lots of luggage—I didn't know that they had changed to a larger car. As we were driving away the driver stated that we had fourteen bags, and I said, "oh, God!" The driver looked up.

"I think Frannie's in the other car!" I said.

"Oh, for God's sake," Tom shouted. "We've left Frannie!"

The whole thing added some levity to a very serious and sad situation.

Frannie's Chicago reception was held in the Great Hall of the Art Institute of Chicago. A big exhibition was opening the next day featuring the artist Christopher Wool, whose work Frannie collected.

Unbeknownst to us, a painting she had lent the exhibit was chosen for the cover of the catalog and as the show's logo. The painting *Trouble*, a white panel with the red letters TRBL, was on every bus, kiosk, and flag all the way down Michigan Avenue. It was surreal, like Frannie was smiling down on us from above.

62

SPIRIT
by Randall C. K. Day

Bill and I moved to Los Olivos in October of 2008 from the New York City area, where I was the rector of another St. Mark's Episcopal Church, in Teaneck, New Jersey. It's funny when you enter a community that is already in motion in every way; you step in and assume that everyone has been there forever. That was around the time that Frances Schultz was starting her life here with Tom, but we didn't realize that at the time.

The first time we met Tom was when we were invited with Kate and Brooks Firestone to Rancho La Zaca for Sunday supper. When we left we thought, *Well, that was lovely. But that's that.* The next Sunday, Frances invited us again and it was just the four of us and our dog, Ike, and Tom's dog, Stella. We arrived at six. When it got to be about nine, Tom looked at us and said, "Now, either we're going to go outside and smoke cigars and get drunk, or you're going home." We said we're going home. It became a thing and it established our Sunday suppers. It works well for all of us.

Tom presents as a large character on one hand, and on the other hand he makes it easy for people to come into his presence. He's courtly and manners are important to him, but he's not formal or stiff. It's what etiquette is meant to do: make it easy for people getting together. He's always impeccably dressed, whether he's in jeans and a sweater, or a suit and a beautiful tie. I think that goes back to his mother, and also why he was able to serve in the Honor Guard. I've known people who have been in those elite military units and the fastidiousness required defies imagination. Tom's cars are always spotless and full of gas. If the tank is a quarter down, he thinks it's empty.

Tom's dog, Stella, is a window into Tom because of the way he is so smitten with her. When Tom goes to a local restaurant, they ask if he wants Stella's usual, which is either a burger or meatballs. He's so proud telling stories about how she retrieved a bird from the pond, and she's blind! It's like how people tell stories about what their kids did in school that day. He gives himself to the relationship with Stella and it reveals that piece of him that people might not know—that he is sweet and compassionate, and he lives from the heart.

Tom was energetic in the way he did business and he expected the best of the people around him. To me that also expresses a vibrant and vital way of living in the world, and that is part of who God is. Tom is like that. He delights in life.

When Frannie died, Frances and Tom understood immediately that Alexis and Jason were the principal mourners, and no decision was made without their input. Tom and Frances were very active and provided resources and time, but they were consistent and immediate in deferring to the children even though they themselves were also clearly mourning.

Tom is intelligent, present, and constantly connecting. I think his hearing loss is painful for him because he loves to connect with people. When he can't hear, I think it creates a sense of anxiety because he wants that connection. He's a voracious reader and always learning. He

grew up unable to read or communicate well, and yet he's always interested in the people around him. I think that in some way his wealth is
more for the people around him than for himself. He could probably
maintain his life at a much lower price point, but he enjoys giving to
the people around him.

I think he felt disrespected at the end of his marriage to Sandy, and
that didn't play well for him. He was amazed at how self-defeating she
was at the end. He's a man who needs to be married. He needs a focus
for his generosity and someone to delight in life with him. In some
ways it seemed that she was right for him in that she was adventurous
and she always pushed the envelope, but in reality they didn't work as a
couple. At the very, very end of that marriage—the night before his
divorce was final—we were out to dinner at our friends the Ballantines.
This was after four years of a really turbulent time for Tom, and Frances
was in New York, and he was feeling down. It was also just months
before his and Frances' wedding, so he was feeling the pressures of that
as well. It became apparent during dinner that a designated driver would
be a good idea for Tom. He protested. I decided to go for the jugular.

"Tom," I said, "if you live through the night, you will be divorced
tomorrow."

"You're right," he said, and handed me the keys.

He perceives the people around him in an egalitarian way. I see it in
the way he bonds with staff at his ranch. Wyatt, the ranch manager;
Felipe, the vineyard manager; and Stephanie, the chef—they're his
friends. He views them as family. He is responsive to people in need.
He's generous and given to anonymity. He mistrusts, like almost anybody these days, large institutions and governments because he knows
how ineffective they can be.

He doesn't want to be known as a religious person or a spiritual
person, and he would never try to explain who God is. I think he just
assumes there is a God and is just letting God be God.

63

THE LEGACY
by Jason Dittmer

I'm not sure you learn how to be a good husband from watching your dad. I think you learn how to be a good husband by watching your mom. My dad said to me when I was a kid, "Look, son, everything in life you can pretty much reverse. Decisions like where you go to college seem big, but if you don't like it, you can go somewhere else. The only things really irreversible in life are death and the mother of your children. Those things are forever."

When my wife Allison and I had our sons, Casey and Jesse, our entire worldview changed. They are the most important things to me and give me the most joy in the world. I love sharing them with my dad, and he is such a good influence on them, even though he'll say things like, "Well shit, yeah, we can go to the toy store." I mean, sometimes he doesn't have the best judgment when it comes to childcare, but my kids are wonderful with him. He doesn't understand a third of what they say because he's so deaf, but they love being around him.

When I look back at what my dad has accomplished, his Achilles' heel may have been that deep down he didn't believe that he was as smart as he really is. He may have set too much store by someone's pedigree or education. I look back and see Phil and Tone, Oxford and Yale graduates respectively. They didn't have the same integrity that Dad had. Refco might still be around today if Dad had hired someone from the University of Iowa who shared his character and integrity.

All I want is for my dad to be happy. Sometimes I worry he's still searching for something, and I don't know what that is. Maybe he wants to get back to what he once was, but that's crazy to me because he has three beautiful grandchildren, two kids that adore him, a wonderful wife, and a beautiful ranch. Who cares how much money you have? The money isn't going to show up at his funeral. What matters is that he has touched people and made their lives better. I wish for him to think: Wow, not bad for an Iowa farm boy. I did all right. I have people who love me.

64

CONVERGENCE

One of the reasons the commodities markets don't work like they used to is because there's no convergence between the futures price and the cash price. The cash price is what you'd pay if you bought the commodity right now, today. In the old days, if the futures price was lower than the cash, we'd buy up the futures and say we'd take delivery of the cattle. I, and thirty or forty of our brokers, would buy thousands of contracts. That made the Exchange crazy, because the guys actually selling the cattle wanted to hold out for the higher cash price. If we were going to take delivery of the cattle, they either had to deliver, or buy back the contract at a higher price. Boom! The prices converge. It was totally legal, but it pissed everybody off. I'd get called before the Board of Trade just about every time I did it, and I did it every chance I could.

I never understood why they wanted to punish us. The *market* would punish us, and you can only squeeze a market when it's going up. If you're wrong, and the market goes against you, they carry you out in a basket. I've been there plenty of times. But nobody ever mentions that.

Most speculators just speculated. The last thing they wanted was to actually have the cows, or whatever, delivered to their door. But because we had the feedlots, we were able to take delivery. We bought thousands and thousands of contracts, and made millions doing it.

Our great edge, of course, was that we were feeders who could hedge *and* we were speculators. The other big traders, like Cargill, the Kochs, Continental Grain, and Simplot, were different because they didn't have me, a speculator, as a partner. As our Cactus feedlot operation got bigger, we started pushing everybody around a little. That's when the Board of Trade changed the rulebook for feeders and speculators. They went after me six ways from Sunday.

The ironic thing is that in those days, a single broker couldn't own more than 600 cattle contracts at a time. That's why, at Refco, we had to have so many brokers to trade the volume we did. Today a single broker can own thousands of contracts. The rules for speculators and hedgers are different. The hedgers are generally feeders, or sellers or buyers, of actual cattle or beef, who want to hedge against future price swings. A hedger doesn't have to reduce or cover the number of contracts he holds by a certain date, but a speculator does.

The Exchange wants the market to liquidate; they don't want you taking delivery. So in that way the system is rigged to go down because there is a lot of selling as the contract nears its expiration date. Therefore, both the hedgers and speculators were generally short, and they'd both come out okay. They had the downside covered. Meanwhile, the lower futures price more or less converged with the higher cash price.

If there's no convergence, then why have a futures market? That's partly what has happened to the markets in the last few years. There is practically no exchange. There are no people in offices sitting around talking about weather, and blizzards in Montana, and late summers in South Dakota. The old traders died off and, of course, the computers have taken over. Nearly 90-some percent of futures trades are done electronically now.

The Chicago Board of Trade and Chicago Mercantile Exchange merged in 2007 to become the CME Group. Then, in 2015, they closed all but a handful of the live, open-cry trading pits. There's very little volume now, and very little liquidity, but the volatility is tremendous.

It used to be that in an entire year, the price of cattle might fluctuate by $17. Now, you might see a $10-range in just a week. The cash price doesn't move, but the futures do. It's very tough to trade because it doesn't make sense. You can't judge the risk-reward because you don't know how much you could lose. The price fluctuations aren't based on research, or what's actually going on with the world's cattle herd. They're based on momentum trading by computer and algorithm.

It's the same with grains. They used to say rain begets rain, and drought begets drought. Rain makes grain. In 2016, it looked to be the largest soybean crop in history, but the price went from $9 a bushel to $12 because it didn't rain for a couple of days. I talked to my research guys and asked them how this could happen. They said things are different these days. So, you get out. You don't lose any money, but you don't make any money. In the meantime, soybeans went back from $12 to $9, and everyone who didn't get out is now broke. The same thing is happening with corn, but it didn't use to. Once, in '92 or '93, I saw prices getting high, around $3.30 a bushel. Our research said the crop would be big, which meant prices would go down. One night, I had a dream that I was talking to Willard Sparks.

"Willard, where's the corn market going?"

"$3.35," he said.

I woke up in a cold sweat. That dream was so real that the next day I started selling.

"Shuff," I said to Tom Shuff, one of my longtime traders, "sell me 5,000 contracts." He'd come back, and the market would rally. I'd say,

"Shuff, did you fill the goddamn order backward? Did you buy them instead of sell them?"

"No! I sold them to one guy!"

"Sell 5,000 more." Boom!

Sparks calls me up. "What are you doing!?"

"Willard, I woke up last night in a cold sweat. Where's the corn market going?"

"Let's see. Now, it's trading at $3.30," he says. "It's gonna go to three thirty-ffff—" *Click*. He hung up and *he* started selling.

Why stay for the last nickel of the rally? It's fucking crazy! And the market did go up another nickel. The next day, though, it opened limit down. We couldn't sell anything.

That couldn't happen today because the liquidity has evaporated. I'd sell 25,000 corn contracts at a time, and the market would keep right on going. Today, I'm not sure you could buy or sell 25,000 contracts in an entire day.

So much of the trading today is based on algorithms and technical factors. High-frequency traders exacerbate that by canceling orders microseconds after placing them. That's happening in the stock markets, too, and that's what Michael Lewis wrote about in his book *Flash Boys*. It has a distorting effect on the markets, and nobody knows how to trade or what to do. I don't, anyway. Those days are gone.

65

MY BEST ADVICE AND MY GREATEST WEAKNESS

Like Teddy Blue said, "When a cowboy is too old to set a bad example, he hands out good advice." Here's some good advice.

Life is a painting and you're Picasso. Every day you get to put a few strokes on the canvas, so make sure they're good strokes. That goes for everything.

The best personal advice I ever got was from my mother. She told me the woman I marry would be the most important decision I would ever make. Therefore, don't go out with the town whore. I might marry any one of the girls I dated, so I'd better only date nice, marriageable women.

And never lower the bar so you can step over it.

I'm from Iowa, I was a bad student, I stuttered, and I had no prospects. So when I started to make money in Chicago, I thought, "If I can do it, anybody can do it." I started giving people money and helping them out and that just didn't work. That was my greatest weakness, and I made a tremendous number of bad decisions because of it. I finally learned that the most valuable thing I could ever do for people was to give them an opportunity to show what they could do.

When I hired people I would say, "We want to go from point A to point B in building the business. That's the direction." I wouldn't tell them how to do it; they had to think it up. I trusted them to take the initiative. This was my business and if the people who worked for me were for me, then it worked.

No one gives a shit about the president of the company; it's the people on the floor who make the business. The secretaries and the people that worked for me were superstars, all of them. A major part of my success came from hiring the best people. Character is the most important thing to me and I always tried to surround myself with people of character. I was accused of cheating many times, but I never cheated. I just did my homework and I pushed the envelope as far as I could.

Before we were completely computerized, our volume was so big that we had five or six smart, young kids who used to sleep on the office floor at night. They wanted to get their work done and be there in the morning. No one told them to do it; they did it because I trusted them. We were able do what we did at Refco because of the people.

There is an ego trip that comes with being the biggest cattle feeder, the biggest clearinghouse, and a bigger futures trader than the Board of Trade. When I walked into the annual dinner at the Exchange, I was the biggest guy in the room. But I was also the biggest target; they go together.

The ego trips, the money, the fancy things, the adventures were all fun, but they're not the source of my pride. What I'm most proud of in my life is that I have two great kids, and because of that my grandchildren will be great and they'll make the world better.

I'm also proud that I was able to have so many great friends in my life. I still get together with friends I had from college, from the Army, and from Refco. The people that Frannie and I had a thousand wonderful times with—traveling all over the world, going to dinners, having parties—thousands of silly, fun times. One of my friends died recently and I cried because it hit me that when an old friend dies, a part of your life has died with him.

I was blessed with my mother and Pop. I was blessed that I had Frannie in my life; there was no one like her. I am blessed with my wife Frances, and we have a wonderful life together.

Remember, I'm not supposed to be here. I'm supposed to be in Sioux City driving the Coke truck on my best day. The fact that I stumbled out and got to do what I did is a miracle.

Not bad for an Iowa farm boy.

ACKNOWLEDGMENTS

This book happened because I was cajoled and occasionally outright bullied into it by my otherwise adorable wife, Frances, who is also a damn good writer and editor. She and Skyhorse editor Mark Weinstein crafted and cut this crazy string of stories into what I hope is a readable crazy string of stories. Thank you. I think.

Casey DeFranco, friend, author, and candidate for sainthood, did the yeoman's work of interviews with yours truly and others, and wrangled them into a coherent structure. She also cleaned up my language. By a lot. Thanks, Casey.

Thank you to longtime friend Jeff Pill for the connection to Skyhorse Publishing and Skyhorse editorial director Jay Cassell, to whom I am also grateful. Thank you also to Skyhorse editor Veronica Alvarado. This book was initially going to be seven self-printed copies for my children and grandchildren. I'm still not quite sure how this publishing thing happened.

I am deeply grateful to all the people at Refco with whom I had the pleasure of working for thirty years, especially Willard Sparks, who took our business to the next level. In the cattle business, Paul Engler lead me into a great partnership and a lifelong adventure.

For taking their time to speak with Casey and share their stories in these pages, I am grateful to my children Jason and Alexis; cousin Susan Robertson for her help with photos and family research; my former assistants Shari Ardhaldjian and Kim Sherman; former Refco guys Tom Scichili and Chris Sugrue; the Reverend Randall Day and his husband Bill Hurbaugh; and to Jeanette Butala and Paul Adams of the Providence St. Mel School, which, next to my family and Refco is the best thing I've ever been involved with. It is my honor that the proceeds from this book are donated to the Providence St. Mel School in Chicago.

Thanks also to the dear friends who read this manuscript and set me straight when necessary, including Charlotte Beers, Memrie Lewis, Rick Kaplan, and Jeff Pill.

And finally thank you to *Rancho la Zaca* manager, cowboy, and executive assistant Wyatt Cromer for keeping the home fires burning and putting up with me. Boom.

ABOUT THE AUTHOR

Thomas Henry Dittmer, a legendary figure in the Chicago and New York commodities and trading world, was born in 1942 in Hawarden, Iowa, and raised in Sioux City. A University of Iowa graduate, Dittmer served as a member of the US Army's prestigious 3d Infantry "Old Guard," and was a White House social aide under Lyndon B. Johnson. With his stepfather Raymond E. Friedman, Dittmer co-founded the erstwhile brokerage firm Refco, in Chicago, which in its heyday was the largest commodities brokerage firm in the world. Dittmer was also a partner with Paul Engler in Cactus Feeders Inc., then the world's largest cattle feeding operation. Upon his retirement from Refco in 1999, Dittmer for several years ran a successful hedge fund in New York and continues as an active private investor today. He has been involved in numerous philanthropic causes, notably the Providence-St. Mel School in Chicago's West Side. With his first wife, the late Frances Ronshausen Dittmer, Dittmer has a son, a daughter, and three grandchildren. He and his wife, writer Frances Schultz, live on a ranch in the Santa Ynez Valley of Southern California.